W9-DHU-481

Profiles in Two-Way Immersion Education

Donna Christian
Christopher L. Montone
Kathryn J. Lindholm
Isolda Carranza

Center for Applied Linguistics and Delta Systems

CARL A. RUDISILL LIBRARY
LENOIR-RHYNE COLLEGE

©1997 by the Center for Applied Linguistics and by Delta Systems Co., Inc. All rights reserved. No part of this book may be reproduced, in any form or by any means, without permission in writing from the publisher. All inquiries should be addressed to Delta Systems Co., Inc., 1400 Miller Parkway, McHenry, IL 60050-7030.

Printed in the United States of America
10 9 8 7 6 5 4 3 2

Language in Education: Theory and Practice 89

Editorial/production supervision: Jeanne Rennie
Copyediting: Jeanne Rennie
Production: Amy Fitch
Interior design: Sonia Kundert
Cover: Vincent Sagart

ISBN 1-887744-05-3

L C
3 73 J
. P 76
/ 997
m uy 2000

A 8 L 37 J 3

This book was prepared for publication with funding from the Office of Educational Research and Improvement, U.S. Department of Education, under contract No. RR 93002010. The opinions expressed herein do not necessarily reflect the positions or policies of OERI or ED.

Library of Congress Cataloging-in-Publication Data
Profiles in two-way immersion education / Donna Christian ... [et al.].
      p.   cm. -- (Language in education ; 89)
      "Prepared by the ERIC Clearinghouse on Languages & Linguisitics."
      Includes bibliographical references (p.).
      ISBN 1-887744-05-3 (pbk.)
      1. Education, Bilingual--United States--Case studies.
2. Immersion method (Language teaching)--Case studies. 3. Language arts (Elementary)--United States--Case studies.   I. Christian, Donna.   II. Center for Applied Linguistics.   III. ERIC Clearinghouse on Languages and Linguistics.   IV. Series.
LC3731.P76   1997
370.117'5'0973--dc21   97-889
                                                                                        CIP

Contents

Preface

The discussion of two-way immersion education in this volume is based on research conducted for a study, "Two-Way Bilingual Education: Students Learning through Two Languages," for the National Center for Research on Cultural Diversity and Second Language Learning (1990-1995). This Center was funded by the Office of Educational Research and Improvement of the U.S. Department of Education to conduct research on the education of language minority students in the United States. It was operated by the University of California, Santa Cruz, through the University of California's statewide Linguistic Minority Research Institute, in collaboration with a number of other institutions nationwide, including the Center for Applied Linguistics. Major themes explored by that research group are continuing under the successor federal grant for the Center for Research on Education, Diversity, and Excellence (CREDE), also headquartered at the University of California, Santa Cruz (1996-2001).

The project would not have been possible without the support and cooperation of the teachers who were observed and interviewed. We know that it was difficult having researchers sit in their classes and collect information about teaching strategies and student interactions. We extend our sincere appreciation to the teachers involved, as well as to the students, who willingly answered our questions and tried to interact normally with tape recorders running and people around them taking notes.

We are especially grateful to representatives of the three programs profiled here who helped us arrange our school visits and provided us with large amounts of information. We called on individuals who had far too much to do already to give their time and energy to this effort, and we appreciate their assistance. From Francis Scott Key Elementary School, Arlington, VA: Katharine Panfil, Marcela von Vacano, Evelyn Fernández, and Marjorie Myers. From River Glen Elementary School, San Jose, CA: Rosa Molina, Linda Luporini-Hakmi, and Cecilia Barrie. From Inter-American Magnet School, Chicago, IL: Eva Helwing and Maria Cabrera. We hope that they will find the results useful.

We would like to express our gratitude to Patrick Proctor, who spent considerable time at River Glen observing teachers and students interacting as well as interviewing teachers. We also benefitted from the assistance and consultation of a number of our colleagues who helped us throughout the study. Our thanks go out to Cindy Mahrer, Anna Whitcher, Susan Barfield, Elizabeth Howard, Fred Genesee, Merrill Swain, Dick Tucker, Nancy Rhodes, Deborah Short, and Lupe Silva for their contributions and ongoing support for the project. While we take sole responsibility for the contents of this volume, we gratefully acknowledge the input and time commitment of those who reviewed the manuscript and offered suggestions that have improved it: Sue Baker, Elizabeth Howard, Mimi Met, Jeannie Rennie, and Dick Tucker.

Donna Christian
Christopher L. Montone
Isolda Carranza
Center for Applied Linguistics

Kathryn J. Lindholm
San Jose State University
September 1996

The work reported herein was supported under the Educational Research and Development Centers Program, PR/Award Number R117G1002, as administered by the Office of Educational Research and Improvement, U.S. Department of Education. However, the contents do not necessarily represent the positions or policies of the Office of Educational Research and Improvement, or the U.S. Department of Education.

This book is dedicated to all the educators and students who are working to foster bilingualism through two-way immersion.

CHAPTER ONE
Introduction

Two-way immersion programs, also referred to as *bilingual immersion* and *two-way bilingual* programs, integrate language minority and language majority students in the same classroom with the goal of academic excellence and bilingual proficiency for both student groups. In these programs, most language instruction is not done directly; rather, as content is learned in the non-native language, that language is also acquired. Two-way programs provide content area instruction in both the non-English and the English language and aim for student academic performance at or above grade level in both languages. An additional goal of many programs is to create an environment that promotes linguistic and ethnic equality and fosters positive cross-cultural attitudes.

Although there are a number of variations among two-way immersion programs, they all share several characteristics. They provide instruction in two languages, with the non-English language typically used for at least 50% of the instructional time. Only one language is used in the classroom at any given time: For some content areas, English is used; for others, the non-English language is used. Finally, native speakers of both English and the non-English language (preferably in balanced numbers) work together in the classroom for most content instruction, serving as resources for one another in both language and content.

The rationale for the basic two-way immersion approach derives from several theoretical assumptions about content learning and language learning. First, content knowledge acquired through one language paves the way for knowledge acquisition in the second language (Collier, 1992; Hakuta & Gould, 1987; Krashen, 1991; Lambert & Tucker, 1972; Swain & Lapkin, 1985; Tucker, 1990). Studies on a variety of bilingual education program models have shown that when native language instruction is provided for language minority students with appropriate second language instruction, students can achieve academically at higher levels in the second language than if they had been taught in the second language only. Thus, students who learn content in one language can be expected to demonstrate content knowledge in the second language, as they acquire the language skills to express that knowledge.

Second, researchers in bilingual education suggest that a second language is best acquired by language minority students after their first language is firmly established (Cummins, 1984; Hakuta, 1987, 1990; Snow, 1987). Development of literacy in a second language appears to occur more slowly if the student's first language literacy skills are weak or nonexistent. As native language literacy develops, it is believed that literacy skills transfer more easily to the second language, although recent research indicates that the transfer of skills is not as straightforward as once assumed (Snow, 1994). Additive bilingualism is attained when the ethnic minority language is maintained along with the prestigious national language, and high-level skills are developed in both languages.

Language majority children (those who are fluent speakers of the high status language in the society, e.g., English in the United States) also benefit from an immersion experience for language learning and do not suffer academically when content instruction is provided via a second language (Harley, Allen, Cummins, & Swain, 1990).

Third, it has become increasingly evident in the decades since the first Canadian language immersion programs were implemented in the 1960s that language is learned best when it is the medium of instruction rather than the goal of instruction (Brinton, Snow, & Wesche, 1989; Chamot & O'Malley, 1994; Crandall, 1995; Genesee, 1987; Harley et al., 1990; Lambert & Tucker, 1972; Met, 1991; Mohan, 1986; Olsen & Leone, 1994; Snow, Met, & Genesee, 1989; Spanos, 1990). Children who learn language as they work on academic tasks engage in purposeful discourse within meaningful contexts. In other words, students explain, describe, solve problems, and ask and answer questions about social studies, math, science, and so forth. In immersion settings, students learn language while learning content, because there is a real need to communicate while engaged in content-related tasks. Immersion students tend to learn language better than those who study the language *qua* language alone. From the evidence available thus far, the immersion experience appears to be appropriate for all language majority students, regardless of their socioeconomic background or achievement level (Genesee, 1992). However, since investigations of this question are quite limited, further study is needed to understand how various factors that place students at risk academically affect their ability to succeed in immersion classrooms.

Finally, sociocultural theory, developed largely out of the work of Vygotsky, also plays a role in supporting the two-way immersion approach. Sociocultural theory holds that language acquisition—as all learning—occurs through social interaction within an immediate social context. Meaningful linguistic input is transmitted to the child during interaction with more experienced speakers. Similar processes appear to be involved in the acquisition of a second language. This feature is built into two-way immersion classrooms, where students have ongoing opportunities to interact with fluent speakers (both teachers and peers) of the language they are learning. Two-way immersion classrooms, then, present a facilitative sociocultural context for learning for both language minority and majority students. From an institutional perspective, this approach offers an additive bilingual environment in its program design and classroom organization; from an interpersonal perspective, it offers opportunities for meaningful interactions with fluent speakers of the languages being learned and close contact with members of diverse cultural groups.

While there has been considerable research on language learning in a variety of settings (Collier, 1992; Genesee, 1987; Hakuta, 1990; Olsen & Leone, 1994), there has been relatively little study of language development in two-way programs, where students can continue to develop their native language as well as benefit from peer interaction with fluent speakers of their second language. Further, since most two-way programs are relatively new, there has been little opportunity to compile and synthesize the knowledge that is being gained.

The purpose of this volume is to begin to document that experience by profiling two-way immersion programs in three schools that are implementing different variations of the model. Our goal is to describe each program's evolution, current operation, and results, drawing comparisons wherever feasible. By examining the programs in some depth, and by highlighting some similarities and differences, we hope to contribute to a greater understanding of how two-way immersion works.

A National Perspective

It is useful to consider the national context before delving into individual program descriptions. During the period 1992 to 1995, we compiled information about two-way immersion programs as they were currently being implemented and evaluated in the United States. The following information was solicited from each program: location and contact information, background information, program and student demographics, instructional approach and design, program staff and professional development, evaluation information, and additional commentary (Christian & Whitcher, 1995).

By 1995, information had been received from 182 schools, in 19 states, who reported that they were implementing two-way programs (see Table 1.1).[1] Most of these programs are at elementary grade levels (149 of the 182 schools) (see Table 1.2). Nearly all two-way programs use Spanish and English as the languages of instruction (167 schools); other languages of instruction include Arabic, Cantonese, French, Japanese, Korean, Navajo, Portuguese, and Russian (see Table 1.3). The majority of programs (about two thirds of the schools) are relatively new (less than six years old) (see Table 1.4), not a surprising fact when one compares these figures with a 1987 study that identified only 30 two-way programs in operation (Lindholm, 1987). Clearly, interest in two-way immersion programs has increased dramatically in recent years.

---

[1] In this count, all schools who reported that they operate a two-way program and offer instruction through two languages for both language minority and language majority students were included. The variation in models and contexts of implementation was tremendous, however, and some features reported would not be widely accepted as characteristics of two-way immersion.

TABLE 1.1

Two-Way Immersion Programs by State

State	Number of Districts	Number of Schools
Alaska	1	1
Arizona	4	8
California	31	58
Colorado	2	5
Connecticut	3	3
District of Columbia	1	1
Florida	2	6
Illinois	3	12
Massachusetts	8	13
Michigan	2	2
Minnesota	1	1
New Jersey	2	2
New Mexico	1	1
New York	28	49
Oregon	1	3
Pennsylvania	1	1
Texas	5	9
Virginia	3	6
Wisconsin	1	1
TOTAL	**100**	**182**

TABLE 1.2

Grade Levels Served in Two-Way Immersion Programs

Grade Levels Served	Number of Schools
Pre-K/K	8
K-6	141
K-8	14
K-12	2
6-9	16
9-12	1
Total	**182**

TABLE 1.3

Languages of Instruction in Two-Way Immersion Programs

Languages of Instruction	Number of Schools
Spanish/English	167
Korean/English	4
Cantonese/English	3
French/English	2
Navajo/English	2
Arabic/English	1
Japanese/English	1
Portuguese/English	1
Russian/English	1
Total	**182**

TABLE 1.4

Year of Establishment for Two-Way Immersion Programs: 1963-1994

Year established	Number of schools	% of total
1989-1994	137	75
1984-1988	21	12
1979-1983	10	5
1974-1978	5	3
1969-1973	6	3
1963-1968	3	2
TOTAL	**182**	**100**

Descriptive information collected from these two-way programs indicates a great deal of variability. They include both neighborhood-based programs and magnet schools that attract students from throughout a district. Some are programs or strands within a school, while others involve the whole school. Further, programs begin at different stages of educational development—pre-K, kindergarten, first grade, upper elementary, middle, and secondary schools—and continue, in some cases, through secondary school. In nearly all cases, participation is voluntary, and parents choose to enroll their children in the program.

Although most programs share similar goals, their designs vary considerably (Christian, 1996). Most programs try to achieve balanced numbers of language majority and language minority students in the classroom so that each group can serve as a resource for the other in the language being learned.[2] Schools try to avoid having language majority students outnumber language minority students; such a situation can lead to greater in-school use of English, which is already reinforced by exposure outside the school.

---

[2] In some programs, students from the two language backgrounds are separated for some or most of their instruction. In those cases, the possibility of working toward a goal of better cross-cultural understanding and communication would appear to be lessened.

The ratio of instructional time in each language varies among programs. There are two major patterns followed in elementary schools, where the vast majority of programs operate. In one, the native language of the non-English background students is used in the early years for nearly all instruction (80-90%); English is introduced and gradually increased as a medium of instruction to roughly 50% by the upper elementary grades. This is referred to here as the "90-10" model. In programs that follow this model, the language majority students have an immersion experience in a second language, while the minority students receive native language instruction with a gradual introduction of English and English-medium instruction.

In the second common pattern, the percentage of instruction in each language is roughly equal from the beginning. In other words, both English and the non-English language are used about 50% of the time. This is referred to here as the "50-50" model. Additionally, many 50-50 two-way programs have English as a second language (ESL) and Spanish as a second language (SSL) components.

In either pattern, the distribution of the two languages may be accomplished by various means. The time for use of English or the non-English language may be defined by teacher, subject, time (divided day/alternate days/alternate weeks), or any combination of these.

Profiles of Two-Way Immersion

To look more closely at practices and outcomes of individual programs, we undertook descriptions of programs at elementary schools with relative longevity in using the two-way immersion approach (seven or more years) and with records of academic success. Because information about programs in action is relatively scarce, it seemed most beneficial to aim at descriptions of the most common context—that is, elementary schools with Spanish/English programs—as a starting point, and to look at schools with a good deal of experience. Within these parameters, the programs selected were geographically diverse and represented the major variations in two-way program design (i.e., 90-10 and 50-50). As mentioned earlier, two-way immersion programs typically work toward at least three goals: language and literacy development in two languages, high academic achievement, and positive cross-cultural attitudes and behaviors. This study focused on the first two and did not collect data directly related to attitudes or other socio-psychological outcomes. Others have found positive results in that area, however (Lambert & Cazabon, 1994; Lindholm, 1994).

For the profiles, we sought to collect information about student development and about the administrative and instructional practices that could contribute to the success of the program. In addition to descriptive information provided by the schools, our data included classroom observations, interviews with teachers and staff, a teacher questionnaire, and student performance measures.

This volume contains profiles of two-way programs at three sites. Two of the sites were local to the authors (Key Elementary School in Arlington, VA, and River Glen Elementary School in San Jose, CA), so observations and contact were possible on a regular basis. At the third site (Inter-American Magnet School in Chicago, IL), data collection was more limited in scope, with less time on site and more long-distance follow-up. To maximize comparability, there was an attempt to keep the data collected similar across sites, but most data were not controlled in that way—particularly student test data, where, for the most part, results were obtained for tests that are normally given; additional testing was not requested.

Classroom observations, interviews, and other data collection were undertaken during school visits. At Key and River Glen, six site visits over two years (1994-1995 and 1995-1996) provided information for the profiles. Each data collection session lasted two to three days; typically, one day was devoted to a single classroom, whose students were followed throughout the day. Classrooms at Grades 1 through 6 were observed, giving an average of three visits total per grade level. At River Glen, a pre-K through Grade 6 school, all classrooms were at the same location; for Key, a K-5 school, the sixth grade class was observed at the receiving middle school.

Site visits provided descriptive data on the environment and inter-actional behavior of teachers, students, and other participants. Class-room observations focused on aspects of the learning environment, strategies used for developing proficiency and literacy in two languages, strategies for negotiating meaning, and teachers' and students' language use. To help focus these observations, six students at each grade level were selected for closer observation (three native Spanish speakers and three native English speakers). When appropriate (for example, during small group work, when only selected students could be followed), the behavior of these students was more closely attended to in both student–student and teacher–student interactions. Oral and written language samples were gathered from these students as examples of language production in the programs.

Interviews were conducted with the principal, the program coordinator, teachers, and teacher aides at each site. These interviews followed protocols aimed at exploring the evolution of the program; perceptions of the strengths of the program and areas needing improvement; beliefs about effective instructional practices and program design elements, particularly related to promoting language learning; and the individual staff member's background and experience. In addition, several teachers at each site completed a written questionnaire, geared at obtaining more detailed information about teaching and learning (both language and content) in the programs.

Data on student performance were also gathered, focused on language learning and academic achievement. For Spanish oral language proficiency, students were rated by teachers on the Student Oral Proficiency Rating (SOPR) at Key and on the Student Oral Language Observation Matrix (SOLOM) at River Glen. The SOPR and the SOLOM are very similar instruments that measure comprehension, fluency, vocabulary, pronunciation, and grammar (rating scales shown in Appendix A). Both Spanish and English language development were assessed by the Language Assessment Scales-Oral (LAS-O), which measure vocabulary, listening comprehension, and story retelling. At Key, these were administered at third grade only, and at River Glen, they were given each year, Grades 1 through 6. Writing samples in both English and Spanish were also obtained for students at both sites.

To consider academic progress, scores were gathered on standardized tests that were administered district-wide. At Key, fourth grade students each year took the *Iowa Test of Basic Skills* (*ITBS*) in English, including subtests on language, mathematics, reading comprehension, social studies, and science. No achievement tests of content in Spanish were administered. At River Glen, data were available from *La Prueba Riverside de Realización Español* for Spanish reading, mathematics, social studies, and science at Grades 1-6; at Grades 3-7 the *Comprehensive Test of Basic Skills (CTBS)* provided data for English language, reading, and mathematics.

The scope of data gathering was more restricted for Inter-American, because that site was added later in the project and was more distant, but it resulted in sufficient information to prepare a comparable profile for this volume. Two site visits were made: a three-day visit in May 1995, followed by a half-day visit in November 1995 for extension and clarification. Six classrooms at Grades 1, 3, and 5 were observed during routine instruction, and interviews were conducted with the principal, program coordinator, four teachers, and a founding parent/teacher, now working in the District's bilingual education office.

Student language and academic outcomes were assessed on several measures. Spanish reading and writing scores for Grades 3-8 were provided by *La Prueba Riverside de Realización en Español.* The other major source of student outcome data was the Illinois Goals Assessment Program, required of all students in the state except limited English proficient students with fewer than three years of schooling in this country. Reading, mathematics, and writing are tested Grades 3, 6, and 8; science and social sciences are tested in Grades 4 and 7.

In the following chapters, profiles of each site are presented, reporting on the descriptive and quantitative data obtained for each program. Each chapter discusses the school context, program history, program design, instructional features, and student outcomes. The final chapter discusses the similarities and differences across the programs, matching comparable data from the sites wherever available.

CHAPTER TWO
Francis Scott Key Elementary School Arlington County (VA) Public Schools

Program Information

Program Overview

The two-way immersion program in Arlington, Virginia, is called a *two-way partial immersion program*. It was established at Francis Scott Key Elementary School in 1986 with a first grade class, and one grade was added each year as the initial cohort advanced. Kindergarten was added in 1991. Grades K through 5 are offered at the elementary school; students may continue the program in Grades 6-8 at the middle school, and on into high school at Grades 9 and 10. The program has become very popular district-wide, and two other elementary schools began to offer similar programs in 1992.

In the elementary Key School program, each class includes both native Spanish speakers and native English speakers, as well as a few children who speak another language natively. As Table 2.1 indicates, approximately 50% of instruction is in English and 50% is in Spanish throughout the grades. The language of instruction changes at mid-day. Most classes work with two different teachers, one who teaches in Spanish and one who teaches in English; students change classrooms when it is time to change languages each day. In a few classes, one bilingual teacher teaches the same class all day, using English for half the day and Spanish for the other half. The choice of language of instruction for each academic subject may vary from grade to grade based on the abilities and preferences of the teaching staff.

Table 2.1

50-50 Program Design by Grade Level at Key

Grade Level	% of Instruction in Spanish	% of Instruction in English
Kindergarten-Fifth	50	50

Program Goals

The goals of Key's partial immersion program[3] are primarily academic and linguistic. The academic aim is for students to meet or exceed the achievement levels of students in non-immersion classes. At the same time, the program attempts to provide students with a strong background in Spanish to ensure the development of a high level of proficiency. The program also aims to develop positive cross-cultural attitudes and behaviors and high levels of self-esteem.

District and School Characteristics

In 1995, the Arlington Public Schools consisted of 19 elementary schools, 6 middle schools, and 4 high schools serving a total of 17,031 children. Table 2.2 displays the ethnic diversity of Arlington students. Approximately 40% of them come from communities where a language other than English is spoken, and 30% of them are Hispanic. The district had 3,203 limited English proficient (LEP) students in 1995, or 19% of the total school population. Many of these students' second language development needs were served through English for Speakers of Other Languages (ESOL) and High Intensity Language Training (HILT) programs at all educational levels. Other students were enrolled in two-way immersion programs at one of three schools. As of 1995, these two-way programs were educating approximately 600 students in both Spanish and English.

---

[3] The school district's term for the program will be used in this section.

Table 2.2

District and Program Characteristics: Percentage of Students from Different Ethnic Backgrounds, on Free Lunch Program, and Limited English Proficient (1995)*

	District (17,000 students)	Immersion Program at Key (300 students)
Ethnic Background		
Hispanic	30%	48%
European American	42%	46%
African American	18%	5%
Asian American	9%	1%
Native American	0	0
Free/Reduced-Price Lunch	38%	34%
Limited English Proficient	19%	40%

*All figures are rounded.

In 1995, Francis Scott Key Elementary School had a linguistically and culturally diverse population of 698 students in Grades K-5. Approximately 40% of Key's students were limited English proficient. Many received instruction in ESOL or HILT programs. Others were among the Spanish language background students in the two-way immersion program.

Nearly half of the students at Key were enrolled in the immersion program, which consisted of four classes at kindergarten, three each at first and second grades, two each at third and fourth grades, and one at fifth grade. The program is open to any child in Arlington who is interested, with preference given to students in the Key neighborhood. There is a waiting list, and students with siblings in the program are given priority for admission. The rest of the candidates are chosen on a first-come, first-served basis, taking into account such variables as grade, gender, and native language to maintain an appropriate balance.

In 1994-95, there were 318 students in the Key immersion program: 47% native Spanish speakers, 51% native English speakers, and 2% native speakers of another language. Forty percent were considered limited English proficient when they began the program. Approximately 50% lived outside the school's boundaries (but within the school district) and were bused to Key. Eighteen percent of those bused were native Spanish speakers, and 81% were native English speakers (Barfield, 1995).

There were more gifted and talented students in the immersion classes than in Key's regular classes. (Although the immersion program originally began as a program for gifted and talented students, it is now viewed by the school as a program for all students. In the initial stages of the program, school officials felt it necessary to label it a gifted and talented program in order to attract enough students.) During the period the program was observed for this study, there were approximately 3-6 gifted students in each immersion class and 2-3 in each non-immersion class. The average class size in the immersion program was 23 students.

Total African-American enrollment in the program was 4.7% (15 students); total Asian representation was 1.6% (5 students). These were smaller percentages than in the school as a whole (African-American 12%, Asian 5%). Percentages for the entire district were 18% African-American and 9% Asian.

The immersion program at Key appears to be including more students with special needs than in the past. From 1994 to 1995, the number of students receiving special education services who enrolled in the immersion program showed a marked increase. This included 13 children with learning disabilities and 20 who were receiving speech therapy. However, the number of children with learning disabilities and those receiving speech therapy in immersion was not as high as those in non-immersion classes.

The socioeconomic status of students in the immersion program was determined by their participation in the free and reduced-price lunch program. It should be noted that this may not be entirely reliable due to the fact that participation in the lunch programs is voluntary. Twenty-five percent of the children in the partial immersion program received free lunches, and 9% received reduced-price lunches.

Immersion class sizes ranged from 17 to 26 students, with an average of 23. Although the primary grades had a fairly even distribution of native English and native Spanish speakers, the percentage of native Spanish speakers increased at each grade level. This is because when children leave the program, their replacements must have enough proficiency in Spanish to succeed academically. Because the proficiency of students in the program increases from grade level to grade level, new students entering the program in the upper grades must be fairly proficient Spanish speakers. Few native English speakers in the upper elementary school grades are sufficiently proficient in Spanish. The program has started to remediate this trend by increasing slightly the number of native English speakers in the lower grades.

History

During the 1980s, Arlington Public Schools offered two programs for language minority students: English to Speakers of Other Languages (ESOL) and High Intensity Language Training (HILT). The ESOL staff became interested in other models and innovations for educating language minority and language majority students. Through a professional development initiative with the Center for Applied Linguistics (funded by the U.S. Department of Education), Arlington administrators and ESOL staff visited a variety of programs serving language minority students, including bilingual programs in Hartford, Connecticut. These visits took place during the 1985-86 school year.

Following these visits, in the spring of 1986, the principal of Key School decided to implement a two-way program at his school the following year to give language minority and language majority students the opportunity to become bilingual. He first sought parental support. As is often the case in starting up a two-way immersion program, it was easier for the Hispanic parents to understand the benefits of this innovative model and be convinced to enroll their children then it was for the English-speaking parents. But by early summer, the principal at Key was able to attract enough parents from each group to start the program with one class of first graders within the school's gifted and talented strand. During the summer, a search was undertaken for teachers with appropriate qualifications; two teachers, one for the English component and one for the Spanish component, were identified. In September 1986, Key's two-way immersion program began.

The program was monitored by the district foreign language supervisor. Staff of the Center for Applied Linguistics (CAL) agreed to provide technical assistance and staff development and to prepare a program review at the end of the school year. The first of many meetings between Key and CAL staff took place just before the school year began. A meeting was also held for parents. In addition, teachers and interested parents visited a local bilingual program for language minority students and a local foreign language immersion program (for native English speakers). As a result, staff at Key gained access to a network of local educators who were concerned with similar issues.

The Key School program grew from one class of 18 students in 1986 to 318 students in 1995. The program is viewed as stable by the school district; the community views it as so successful that local parents helped start two new immersion programs in the school district in 1992. As the Key program expanded by adding one grade each year, and information about the benefits of the two-language approach was understood by more Arlington residents, there was an increase in the number of parents seeking out the program. By 1989, when enrollment was opened to anyone in the school district, school administrators no longer needed to recruit new parents; parents were learning about the program by word of mouth and were coming to the school on their own to register their children. In fact, 1989 marked the first time there were more students interested than there were places in the program, and a waiting list was begun as an equitable way to keep track of those who would be next in line for admission. By this time, there was as much interest among non-Hispanic parents as there was among Hispanic parents.

In 1991, Arlington Public Schools received a Title VII Developmental Bilingual Education grant from the U.S. Department of Education to strengthen and expand the Key Elementary School program's capacity to serve a greater number of students, fully develop the curriculum units for all grade levels, improve instructional strategies, and provide increased teacher training. Title VII funds also contributed to the program by providing a half-time Project Specialist, adding a supplemental two-way program at the kindergarten level, providing a Spanish language arts summer school component, establishing a Parent Advisory Committee, and supporting Spanish language and bilingual literacy classes to increase parent involvement.

The two-way immersion program in Arlington County expanded to two other schools—Abingdon Elementary and Oakridge Elementary—in 1992. Since that time, Key Elementary has provided guidance, assistance, and support to the administration and staff at the new sites. The program has also been extended to the middle school. In 1994-95, there were 50 former Key immersion students receiving instruction in Spanish in Grades 6-8 at Williamsburg Middle School. The first class of immersion students had reached 10th grade; many were continuing their Spanish language education at Washington-Lee High School.

Because of the ever-increasing interest in Key's program, school officials decided to expand the program again in the fall of 1993. They added three kindergarten classes (for a total of four) and one class each at first, second, and third grade (for a total of three first, three second, and two third grade classes). There continued to be one class each of fourth and fifth grade. The resultant increase in school enrollment forced Key to establish a satellite site at a school building several miles away. Of the classes mentioned above, two kindergarten classes, one first grade, and one second grade class were conducted at the new site (called "Key West") for two years (1993-1994 and 1994-1995).

In a recent innovation, the program began integrating some students from the ESOL and HILT programs into immersion classes taught in Spanish, such as reading and math, in Grades 4 and 5. The immersion program also began including special education children in these classes. As a result, fourth and fifth grade students in 1994-95 changed classrooms to participate in multi-age reading and math classes according to their ability levels in these subjects. Thus, the immersion program has moved toward serving a more diverse group of students than it did originally.

In the 1995-1996 school year, a restructuring took place within the district, and Key School became exclusively a language-program-oriented school. Since that time, it has housed the two-way immersion students from both Key and Key West, as well as the ESOL/HILT program.

Program Features

Administrative Features

Because Arlington Public Schools has no bilingual education office, the two-way immersion program is overseen by the Foreign Language Supervisor for the district. Daily administrative support for the immersion program, however, is provided at Key School by the Project Specialist (also known as the immersion specialist), a position that was created with Title VII funds from the U.S. Department of Education. The immersion specialist provides academic and moral support to students, families, and teachers; disseminates information to parents and educators; and handles public relations. She also leads the curriculum development efforts for the program. She makes presentations locally and nationally about the Key School immersion program and serves as a resource to other programs in Arlington as well as to educators from around the county and abroad.

Teachers and Staff

The immersion staff at Key School in 1994-1995 included 14 full-time teachers, 3 teacher's aides in kindergarten classes, and an immersion specialist as coordinator of the program. At Williamsburg Middle School, there were two teachers who provided instruction in Spanish for the immersion program. All teachers observed for this study were women. Of the eight teachers who provided information on their professional background during interviews, the average number of years of teaching experience was nine, although there was a wide range, with one first grade teacher in her first year of teaching and a second grade teacher with 23 years teaching experience. Four teachers who provided instruction in Spanish were native speakers, coming from Chile, Colombia, Dominican Republic, and Mexico. The two who were non-native speakers of Spanish had spent considerable time in Spanish-speaking countries—18 years in Colombia for one and several years in Costa Rica for the other. Four teachers had bachelor's degrees, three had master's degrees, and one had a doctorate. Five were certified in elementary education, three in English as a second language, and two in bilingual education. There is no formal requirement for a specific level of Spanish proficiency for those teachers teaching in Spanish who are not native speakers. However, their language proficiency is assessed informally by an administrator during the interview process when they teach a sample lesson to a class.

With regard to the Spanish language skills of teachers teaching in English, the immersion specialist suggested that "it is advantageous for all teachers to be bilingual, including those who teach only in English." It can help their interactions with parents and shows the students that everyone can learn Spanish. "But even more important than the teachers actually speaking Spanish," she explained, "is their demonstration of a positive attitude toward the languages and cultures represented."

Curriculum

Students in the immersion classes are expected to progress academically at the same rate as non-immersion students. At all grade levels, they receive approximately 50% of their academic instruction in Spanish and 50% in English. (See Table 2.3.) Kindergarten students attend the partial immersion program for half the day and Montessori or regular English kindergarten classes the other half of the day. For the most part, science, health, and math are taught in Spanish in all grades, and social studies is taught in English.[4]

---

[4] This distribution may vary slightly due to changes in personnel and attempts to utilize the strengths of individual teachers. For instance, in 1993-94, first grade social studies was taught in Spanish, and math was taught in English. The following year, however, brought a change in personnel, and the distribution conformed once again to the pattern as described.

Table 2.3

50-50 Curriculum Design by Language, Subject, and Grade Level

	Science/ Health	Social Studies	Math	Language Arts
Grades 1-5	Spanish	English	Spanish	Spanish and English
Grade 6	English	Spanish	English	Spanish and English

Language arts (including reading) is taught in both English and Spanish from Grade 1 forward. Special classes (music, physical education, and library) are conducted in English.

The teachers use teacher-made materials in all subjects to supplement textbooks in Spanish, such as *Ciencias* (Silver Burdett) or *Matemáticas* (Silver Burdett & Ginn), that follow the county curriculum. A curriculum guide (Arlington Public Schools, 1992) and units of study for the immersion program, as well as a Spanish immersion language arts curriculum, have been developed by Key School staff. One of the strengths of this program is the continuous development of units of study and curriculum guides.

Ongoing and discrete forms of language assessment are used. The ongoing assessment instruments include student portfolios and unit tests in each subject area. The following discrete assessments are conducted at specific times of the school year:

• evaluation of Spanish writing samples in Grades 1-5

• evaluation of English writing samples in Grades 2-5

• Spanish Oral Proficiency Assessment (SOPA) in Grade 2

• Language Assessment Scales (LAS) in Spanish in Grades 1-3

• CAL Oral Proficiency Exam (COPE) in Spanish in Grade 5

• Student Oral Proficiency Rating (SOPR) in Spanish and English in Grades K-5

- Degrees of Reading Power (DRP) in Grades 2-5
- Iowa Test of Basic Skills (ITBS) in Grade 4
- Virginia Literacy Passport Test in Grade 6

Professional Development

The Project Specialist developed a *Handbook for Teachers and Administrators* to offer guidelines on instructional issues. For example, the handbook suggests strategies to encourage students to use Spanish during Spanish instruction time: (a) establish a reward system, (b) include English-background and Spanish-background children in the same teams, and (c) emphasize the importance of being able to speak another language as well as English.

The handbook encourages continuous consultation among teachers in order to coordinate their teaching and reinforce the content in both languages. Teachers are instructed to work in teams and to meet as often as possible. The organization of teachers' teamwork includes having contact teachers designated for different areas of the curriculum: (a) the gifted and talented program, (b) mathematics, and (c) science.

Immersion teachers also participate in regular in-service sessions. In 1993-1994, teachers attended lectures on topics such as second language acquisition, learning strategies, and enhanced mathematics instruction. During 1994-1995, as part of a teacher development project funded by the National Endowment for the Humanities, 20 immersion and non-immersion teachers from Key School engaged in a comparative study of the works of Mario Vargas Llosa and Eudora Welty, with a focus on developing insights into the similarities and differences between the Latino and Anglo cultures. Program teachers also attended lectures on multicultural literature for children.

Parental Involvement

Key parents are very involved in their children's education. An active Parent-Teacher Association (PTA) operates with parents from both English- and Spanish-speaking backgrounds. The group sponsors fund-raising events and special projects, such as book fairs and arts festivals, throughout the year. A smaller group of parents has also served as an advisory committee to the district's Foreign Language Advisory Committee. These parents have helped the school board consider and decide issues regarding school restructuring, neighborhood school status, and articulation of the immersion program into middle and high school. A handbook for parents (Craig, 1995) was developed by a member of the district's Foreign Language Advisory Committee, based on her study of the Key program (for her doctoral dissertation) and her experience with the parent committee.

Within the PTA, the Hispanic parents have formed a *Comité de Padres Latinos* (CPL) (Latino Parents Committee). The CPL helps Hispanic parents register their children for the school year and for summer school, gives workshops on parenting skills and adult literacy, and involves parents in other school activities. For instance, the CPL has implemented a tutoring program that involves students in upper grades tutoring students in lower grades.

Several parents also work as volunteers in the school, helping students with reading and writing. In addition, two parents write a monthly bilingual newsletter, *Key Notes*, that is sent to all parents, keeping them informed of upcoming events and issues of importance at the school.

Learning Environment

Classroom

Seating arrangements in the immersion classrooms we observed reflected the degree to which teachers tended to organize students into cooperative learning groups for classroom activities. In the upper grades (including at the middle school) and in some of the lower grades observed, the desks were arranged in columns, sometimes in pairs forming two columns, facing the blackboard at the front of the room. In one case, pairs of students faced each other, turning their heads to the side to look at the front blackboard. In the rest of the lower grade classrooms, students were seated in groups of five or six at round or hexagonal tables.

In most classrooms, there were many visual displays; some of those included students' work. In the English classrooms, all displays were in

English. In first and second grade classrooms, there were posters about classroom rules, an upper and lower case alphabet, calendars, a chart showing names of colors, posters of plants and seeds and parts of a plant, and an author-of-the-month display, featuring one of the student's written work. In the back of one classroom, mailboxes of construction paper had been set up for each child. Other displays throughout the year included proofreading guidelines, "I'm an American" rhyme, and lyrics to patriotic songs. In one English classroom there were often sentences on the board with grammatical, lexical, and mechanical errors taken from student work, with the title "What's wrong?". Bookshelves were well stocked with children's reading material in English.

In the Spanish classrooms, most displays were in Spanish (e.g., classroom rules, alphabet, months of the year, number words, colors). There were some books in English. Resources in the classroom included dictionaries and science texts. Homework assignments were written on the board in Spanish.

In Grades 3-6, the displays on the walls reflected the use of the same room for both Spanish and English language instruction (in three cases with the same teacher). There were, for example, science-related items and composition guidelines in English and Spanish. Other resources in the room included math and health books in Spanish, and spelling books, dictionaries literature, a globe, and wall maps in English.

There were numerous lists of learning strategies, cooperative work strategies, writing process steps, and classroom rules. In one sixth grade classroom, many displays were bilingual. In another Spanish sixth grade classroom, there was a poster in English about grammatical categories and several charts of Spanish verbs conjugated in the indicative and the subjunctive moods. There were magazines and books in Spanish.

Because Key's immersion program exists as a program within a school, each day began with the Pledge of Allegiance recited in English over the school's public address system. Students in the immersion program would then repeat the pledge in Spanish. Other school announcements were usually made in English.

Library Resources

In 1995 the library contained over 17,000 volumes, with Pre-K-Grade 2 materials on the lower floor and resources for Grades 3-5 on the upper floor. About 5% of the school's holdings are in Spanish. The Spanish and bilingual books are integrated with the English books by subject matter and are indicated with a sticker on the binding that reads "Spanish." About half a dozen sets of reference materials are available in Spanish, mainly for the upper grade students, including encyclopedias and dictionaries. The immersion program also enjoys a larger set of materials in Spanish that were acquired several years ago through other funds dedicated specifically for this purpose; this special collection was not counted among the library's general holdings. In general, the school has had trouble finding appropriate Spanish-language materials for the educational level of the students and at reasonable prices. However, the library has plans to expand its Spanish-language holdings in the next several years.

Technology Resources

In 1995, Key's computer lab consisted of 19 Macintosh computers, 9 printers, and 1 scanner. Software included a site license for the *Bilingual Writing Center* for word processing, 10 copies of *Sticky Bear Reading* in English and Spanish, and about 5 CD-ROM stories in English. Individual classrooms varied in how frequently they used the computers. Some used them as often as once a week, while others used them once a month. The most frequent use of computers was for word processing in Spanish and English. Grade 3-5 classrooms used the computers the most, often for writing research reports, stories, or material and graphics for group projects.

Instructional Strategies

Separation of Languages

Key's *Handbook for Teachers and Administrators* strongly discourages concurrent use of both immersion languages, either by consecutive translation or code-switching. During observations, all teachers largely remained faithful to the separation of languages, speaking Spanish only during Spanish time and English only during English time. The handbook states that during Spanish time, "98% of the instructional time should be in Spanish"; however, it leaves room for a flexible application of this policy, especially in kindergarten and the early grades. During the period this program was observed, even when students spoke to the teacher in the non-target language (almost all instances involved students speaking English during Spanish time), the teachers responded in the target language only. If the students knew how to express all or most of what they wanted to say in Spanish, for example, the teacher would often prompt them for Spanish by saying something like *"Cómo?"* ("What?"). Or she might begin to model the utterance in Spanish, which elicited a repetition of the utterance by the individual student in Spanish, with the teacher filling in and modeling the unknown words, conjugations, or construction. If the students still did not know how to express what they wanted to say in Spanish, the teacher would usually model the Spanish for them, occasionally asking the individual student, or sometimes the entire class, to repeat after her.

Language Development Strategies

Many of the strategies used to make content clear and comprehensible (see next subsection below) also were helpful in developing students' language. For example, hands-on and cooperative activities provided many opportunities to practice and use language for meaningful purposes. Big books, songs, science experiments, and other manipulatives gave visual and physical dimensions to new vocabulary and promoted practice of new words and grammatical structures. Students at all grade levels and across most content areas were encouraged to write and to be aware of the process of writing in both languages. Reading in both languages was essential to acquiring subject matter knowledge and was further reinforced in some classrooms by regular sustained silent reading time.

One aspect of the curriculum that teachers were beginning to take a more critical look at in the second year of the observation period was the role of formal language instruction. Following the original philosophy of immersion instruction, Key teachers previously had not been teaching explicitly the patterns of grammar in Spanish. However, after noting some persistent grammatical errors in students' spoken and written Spanish, upper grade teachers in 1994-1995 began to incorporate formal grammar teaching into their language arts instruction. For example, during a lesson, students' attention might be drawn to the patterns of agreement between nouns and verbs, with activities designed to practice use of those patterns. This follows the trend in other immersion programs (Day & Shapson, 1996) to teach formal rules of the immersion language as part of the curriculum.

Making Content Comprehensible

In classrooms where students are learning through a language other than their mother tongue, it is essential that teachers make content clear to all students. In two-way immersion classrooms where students are fully integrated, every session involves some students learning content through their non-native language. Because there are teachers in the program who speak only English, they might not always understand their limited English proficient students. Such a scenario was not observed at Key, most likely because many of the native-Spanish-speaking children enter the immersion program knowing at least some English. Nevertheless, in such situations, teachers may ask another student in the class to interpret the limited English proficient student's utterance. The teacher may also ask other students to explain something to limited English proficient students who are having trouble understanding her.

The teachers observed employed a variety of strategies to make content comprehensible. Manipulatives, graphic organizers, and visual support (e.g., overhead projector, blackboard, realia, show and tell) were utilized on a daily basis, such as during an earth science lesson when third grade students used a flashlight and a ball to act out the concepts of rotation and revolution. Abundant visual displays in all rooms served as models of language, references, and reinforcement. In the first grade, students were encouraged to refer to displays as models for their writing. Kinesthetic activities (e.g., mini-dramas, miming, Total Physical Response) were also used frequently.

The teachers used a range of means to check student comprehension of language and content. One first grade teacher utilized physical response activities to check aural comprehension during instruction in English; her Spanish counterpart reviewed each student's written work as soon as it was completed. In third grade, one teacher had students do oral presentations and then ask and answer each other's questions; thus, she was able to monitor the presenter's and other class members' comprehension of the topic. In the upper grades, teachers relied more on student requests for clarification. Whether these clarifications were provided by their classmates or by the teacher varied according to the teacher's individual style.

Teachers generally spoke clearly and at a slightly slower pace in the lower grades (1-3) and during explanations of instructions or new material. This was especially the case during Spanish instruction. In the upper grades, teachers tended to speak at a natural pace. Additional strategies aimed at making meaning clear and modeling language were repetition, rephrasing, paraphrasing, and leading. Teachers also encouraged students to help each other by providing answers, explanations, and modeling language forms.

Little explicit correction of students' linguistic errors was observed in the classrooms. Rather, teachers usually accepted student responses and either modeled the appropriate language or rephrased, paraphrased, or extended the student's utterance, thereby serving as a model. In some cases, the teacher would model the language and ask the student or the entire class to repeat. This was usually done with individual unfamiliar words. Correction of written work was not observed very often, though in many cases this probably took place after school hours.

With regard to language input, the English-speaking teachers offered students native speaker models of oral and written English. In their speech, they exhibited a range of vocabulary and grammatical structures that broadened as grade levels increased. A possible exception was one lower grade teacher's use of a variety of idiomatic expressions. It was not clear whether the students were able to comprehend them all. An upper grade teacher also included quite a few idiomatic expressions in her speech, but at the higher grade level such usage seemed more likely to extend the students' language development than impede comprehension.

Most Spanish-speaking teachers provided highly fluent models of Spanish, exemplifying several regional standard varieties of the language. In some cases, American English influences on Spanish could be detected in syntax (e.g., adjectives before instead of after the nouns they modify) and lexicon (e.g., *colectar*, which does not exist in most varieties of Spanish, for *recoger*, "to collect"). There was also some variation in the Spanish proficiency levels of nonnative Spanish-speaking teachers.

Student Grouping

In the classes observed, cooperative pair or small group work was used extensively. Numerous grouping strategies were utilized, including mixed ability, mixed language background, homogeneous by reading level, and spontaneous groupings by student preference. Cooperative learning in heterogeneous (mixed language background) groups gives students an opportunity to interact in meaningful ways with peers who are fluent in the language they are learning. As a result, students have numerous language models besides the teacher, as well as experiences that help promote the social goal of fostering student respect for other cultures and peoples. In addition, they have many more chances to use the language they are learning.

Student Language Use

Separation of Languages

The students remained faithful to the separation of languages almost always when speaking directly to the teacher and most of the time when performing academic tasks. Among all students, use of Spanish during English time was infrequent and usually limited to an occasional word or phrase. This was true even in the first grade.

In most Spanish classrooms, however, cases of students addressing the teacher in English during Spanish time were observed (especially in the lower grades), and English was used frequently in all grades whenever the teacher was not present or was not the direct addressee. English was the predominant language among students in classrooms where they did not fear being punished for using English during

Spanish time. The promotion of Spanish usage through creative incentives (e.g., make-believe games in lower grades and competitions in upper grades) helped counteract this trend temporarily. Use of English for social purposes by all students during Spanish time seemed to be equally preponderant in all grades.

In most cases, when teachers became aware of the students' use of the inappropriate language, they issued a reminder. This was not done as often or as consistently in the lower grades. The first grade teacher, for example, did little to discourage the students when they used English during Spanish time, but she did occasionally try to promote the use of Spanish as a sort of game to be played during that portion of the day. Overall, the teachers' observed behavior in the classrooms was consistent with what they reported in interviews that they would recommend a teacher do in similar situations.

Second Language Fluency and Accuracy

For students from both language backgrounds, it was apparent that their bilingual skills and abilities increased with each year in the program. Monolingual English-speaking children moved from comprehension to production in Spanish in the early years, then gradually expanded their vocabulary and control over the conventions of the language in the later years. Native Spanish-speaking and bilingual children advanced quickly and steadily in comprehension and production skills in English; by third grade there was little observable difference between them and their native English-speaking peers.

The native Spanish-speaking first graders appeared to be quite comfortable with English, although in the class observed they were not required to speak much. The teacher usually asked for volunteers, so it is difficult to judge the level of English of those who did not speak up. In Spanish, a few native English-speaking first grade students achieved at very high levels, in some cases completing their assignments faster than native Spanish speakers.

All second graders appeared to be quite comfortable with spoken English. In Spanish, advanced language learners were able to construct complete sentences. A few still did not speak much in Spanish (during our observations) but appeared to comprehend oral and written Spanish. Student writing in English and Spanish still included invented spelling, perhaps more so among some native Spanish speakers. The English teacher taught language arts daily, and her stated goal was to eradicate invented spelling by the end of the year. Language arts was not taught separately from content in Spanish on a regular basis.

Among the third graders there was little difference in language groups with regard to English language fluency. Native Spanish speakers would occasionally overuse definite articles (e.g., "When you save the money, you can have a bargain") or fail to invert the subject and verb in embedded questions (e.g., "I don't know what's ping-pong"). In general, though, non-standard grammar or word order in English by native Spanish speakers resembled structures that native English speakers would and did also use (e.g., omission of subject-verb inversion in embedded questions). In Spanish, the native English speakers had achieved a reasonable degree of communicative competence. They were comfortable communicating basic content information, although their speech was somewhat slower and more stilted than that of their native Spanish-speaking peers and included some non-standard grammar and English lexicon. The native Spanish speakers sometimes varied from standard grammar, too, but overall they were noticeably more fluent in Spanish than the native English speakers.

Among the fourth graders, it was difficult to distinguish between the Spanish-background and English-background students when they spoke in English. In Spanish, although they experienced vocabulary limitations, the English speakers had a greater degree of fluency than students in lower grades. Explicit language arts instruction was provided in the 1994-1995 academic year, and the students demonstrated better command of verb inflection patterns. In addition, the students seemed to know how to use some verbs in the preterit tense. They also had begun to use object pronouns, though they did not always position them correctly.

Among the fifth graders, the Spanish-background and English-background groups could not be distinguished from each other in terms of their oral mastery of English. In Spanish, the English-background speakers enjoyed a high degree of fluency, although they still did not match the broader vocabulary of their native Spanish-speaking peers. Incorrect word choice and errors of agreement in number and gender still occurred. (Interestingly, some Spanish-background speakers made the same errors as the English speakers.)

The principal stated, in an interview, that she would like to increase the level of Spanish proficiency. The immersion specialist, noting comments by middle school Spanish teachers concerning fossilized errors, said that more explicit grammar instruction had been added to the fifth grade Spanish language arts curriculum. (The need for increased focus on form has been recognized in other language education programs and is currently being discussed and debated [Harley, 1993]). Further, several aides and teachers interviewed expressed the concern that there were not enough opportunities to use Spanish during the day to ensure higher levels of proficiency, given that electives (e.g., art, music, physical education) were in English and the students were surrounded by English when they left the school. Reflecting on the possibility of moving toward a 90-10 model of immersion, where more Spanish is offered in the earlier grades and slowly decreases to a 50-50 ratio, the principal stated that there was strong community preference, both among English-speaking and Spanish-speaking parents, for keeping the 50-50 model.

Student Written Work

In the fall of 1993, Spanish and English writing samples were collected from the portfolios of eight students—four third graders and four fifth graders. At each grade level, two of the students were native Spanish speakers and two were native English speakers. In the spring of 1995, Spanish writing samples were collected from the same students, and English writing samples were collected from the Spanish-speaking sixth graders.[5]

Analyses of these selected student essays in English and Spanish revealed that, overall, the essays were quite strong with regard to organization, with greater sophistication evident in the upper grade

---

[5] An analysis of focal student writing at Key School was undertaken as part of this project by Elizabeth Howard, a doctoral candidate at Harvard University at the time this research was conducted.

samples. Regardless of the genre or language, the essays contained a topic sentence, supporting details, and a conclusion. Similarly, all of the essays were quite good from the standpoint of mechanics. Spelling errors were infrequent in each language, regardless of the language dominance of the student. The spelling errors that did appear did not seem to reflect any pattern of phonetic confusion between the two languages. This may be due to the fact that there is a great deal of overlap in the mechanics of the languages. Where Spanish differs from English is where the difficulties in student work appeared. Inverted punctuation, for example, was missing in all but a few essays, and accent marks were frequently missing, even in essays written by fifth and sixth grade Spanish-dominant students. In these areas, the students may benefit from the increased direct instruction that has been implemented in the Spanish language arts curricula.

Code-switching, although quite rare, only occurred in the Spanish essays. No children used Spanish words in their English essays; however, there were occasions when both native English speakers and native Spanish speakers incorporated English words into their Spanish essays. This finding is consistent with the observations of oral language use in the classrooms. Interestingly, the code-switches in the writing samples were always flagged by quotation marks, which seems to indicate intentionality on the part of the writer.

In general, the English writing samples were of higher quality than the Spanish writing samples, regardless of grade level or native language of the student. In other words, the English writing ability of students in the program did not seem to be negatively affected by their having received 50% of their academic instruction in Spanish. The 1993-1994 evaluation of the program (Barfield & Rhodes, 1994) reached a similar conclusion. Indeed, the evaluation concluded that dual language instruction seemed to have had a positive effect, given that all classes in the two-way immersion program scored higher than comparable non-immersion classes on the county-wide assessment of English writing.

To illustrate the type of writing produced in the second language, two writing samples by fourth graders are reproduced here. The first is an essay written by a fourth grade native English speaker toward the end of the 1995-1996 academic year.

Irlanda

Irlanda es un país en Europa debajo de Inglaterra. Es divido en dos partes: Irlanda y norte Irlanda. Norte Irlanda es parte de Gran Brittanica.

La tierra de Irlanda es muy fertile y plantas crecen bueno. La papa es el comida principal. Hay muchos campos en Irlanda y mucha de la gente pesca. Tambien es muy frió.

La idioma de Irlanda es Gaelic. Mucho inglés es hablado tambien. Hay muchas ciudades y el capital es Dublin. Otro ciudades son Galway y Belfast.

Irlanda es un isla muy bonita norte y sur.

Erin go bra!

(isla toda las dias)

[Ireland

Ireland is a country in Europe underneath England. It's divided into two parts: Ireland and Northern Ireland. Northern Ireland is part of Great Britain.

Ireland's land is very fertile and plants grow good. The potato is the main food. There are many fields in Ireland and many people fish. It's also very cold.

The language of Ireland is Gaelic. Much English is also spoken. There are many cities and the capital is Dublin. Other cities are Galway and Belfast.

Ireland is a very pretty island north and south.

Erin go bragh!

(island every day)]

The next sample is an English essay written by a native-Spanish-speaking fourth grader at the same time of the year.

Jamestown

Because of the Indians, the store house put on fire and mosquitos the capital Jamestown was moved by the colonists to Wiliamsburg. The colonists thought nobody owned the land because they did not see anybody. However there were people who owned the land, they were the Indians, and they were hating the colonists because they were taking their land. The Indians and the colonists made a deal because their men were getting killed.

Student Outcomes

Oral Language Development

Several kinds of test data were collected on the students in Key's immersion program to assess their language development.[6] For the past six years, the Student Oral Proficiency Rating (SOPR) (see Appendix A) has been used by teachers to assess oral language proficiency in Spanish for all immersion students in Grades K through 5. Each student is rated on five categories of oral language proficiency: comprehension, fluency, vocabulary, pronunciation, and grammar. For each category, the student is rated at one of five levels, ranging from 1, indicating little or no ability, to 5, indicating a level of ability equivalent to that of a native speaker of the language of the same age. Table 2.4 shows that students' oral language ability in Spanish progresses rather steadily as they continue in the program.[7] (Students are not formally assessed for language proficiency at the middle school; hence, no similar data are available on the sixth grade students observed in this case study.)

---

[6] For the most part, test scores are from 1995. In the case of the LAS (Table 2.5), no test was administered in 1995, so 1994 scores are presented here.

[7] Students receiving a total score of 19 or higher are considered fluent.

Table 2.4

1995 SOPR Scores (Spanish)*

Grade Level and Language Background	Percent Fluent	Average Score
First Grade:		
Spanish Speakers	88%	23.0
English Speakers	21%	14.0
Second Grade:		
Spanish Speakers	100%	23.4
English Speakers	21%	16.4
Third Grade:		
Spanish Speakers	N.A.	N.A.
English Speakers	N.A.	N.A.
Fourth Grade:		
Spanish Speakers	100%	24.5
English Speakers	43%	19.8
Fifth Grade:		
Spanish Speakers	100%	23.9
English Speakers	43%	19.7

*Ratings were available for only about 70% of Key students.

   Despite receiving only half of their daily instruction in English, Key's immersion students are excelling in English language development. In 1994, the Language Assessment Scales-Oral (LAS-O) was used to measure the students' English language development. The LAS-O measures vocabulary, listening comprehension, and story retelling. According to the program's 1993-94 evaluation report (Barfield & Rhodes, 1994), both native English and native Spanish speakers scored well on the LAS-O, with 78% of the third graders scoring at the highest level (5) and the other 22% at level 4, both levels being considered fluent. It is also interesting to note that there were no significant differences between native-English- and native-Spanish-speaking students.

Academic Achievement

In March of each year, all fourth graders in Arlington Public Schools are administered the Iowa Test of Basic Skills (ITBS) in English. Subtests include vocabulary, reading comprehension, language (spelling, capitalization, punctuation, language usage), work study skills (visual, reference), mathematics (concept, problem solving, computation), science, and social studies. Test results show that students in the immersion program have progressed in academic areas as well as or better than other students at their grade level. A somewhat higher level of achievement might be expected for the students in the program overall, given the higher proportion of students classified as gifted in immersion as opposed to non-immersion classrooms.

The immersion students have scored significantly higher than the national average (expressed as the 50th percentile) for the past three years. As Table 2.5 indicates, the immersion students scored better than their peers in the state and county, and even better than non-immersion students at Key School.[8] These results are especially interesting in light of the fact that the immersion students have often been studying science, social studies, and mathematics in Spanish, while the ITBS is in English. When native and nonnative English speakers are compared, however, the native English speakers overall scored higher in all seven academic areas of the ITBS (Barfield, 1995).

Because Key does not administer standardized tests of content in Spanish, we were not able to compare their performance in Spanish

---

[8] In fact, Barfield (1995) compared 12 fourth grade immersion students with 12 non-immersion students who were matched for gender, ethnicity, socioeconomic status, native language, and English proficiency. On the ITBS, the immersion students in the sample performed significantly better than the non-immersion students on all subtests and had higher composite scores.

with groups elsewhere. However, teacher reports of in-class assessments of content learning through Spanish support the observation that steady progress and good results are obtained.

Table 2.5

1995 Iowa Test of Basic Skills Average Percentiles as Compared to a National Sample (Fourth Graders Only)

	Language	Math	Reading Comprehension	Social Studies	Science
Immersion (Key)	79	93	89	86	84
Non-immersion (Key)	45	68	53	49	66
Arlington County Public Schools	71	81	74	76	79
Commonwealth of Virginia	64	66	61	65	71

Program Impact

The partial immersion program possesses a number of qualities that are believed to contribute to its success. The following are aspects of the program mentioned in interviews with program teachers, aides, and administrators with regard to the program's strengths:

• Balanced ratio of students and teachers by language background; equal efforts to involve parents from each language background.

• Separation of languages; news bulletins in both languages; parent hotline.

• Cooperation between Spanish and English counterparts.

• Integration of ethnic groups.

• Cultivation of self-esteem; respect for bilingualism; respect for others.

The following are summaries or quotations of comments made by program teachers and administrators with regard to the program's strengths:

- Important components for success have been the time and money that have been donated to the program by LULAC, the *Comité de Padres Latinos*, and other community members.

- "I definitely think it is important that everything be in Spanish in the classroom. That keeps the confusion down and stuff. And I also think that it's good for Spanish to be valued in the school, . . . 'cause lot of time they're [Spanish-background students] not proud that they know Spanish."

- "The expectations are high. We like to have our students do well and we demand a lot of work from them, and we make it in such a way that they enjoy it. So I think that the results are good because they know we expect them to work well, and they have our support. Most of them have support at home. The parents are very supportive of their work, of the program, and of the things we do and ask them to help us with."

- The program is constantly evolving: [about bottom-up decisions and the possibilities for the teachers to experiment with improvements] "I feel good about the program because we are always at the door to see what is out there, but things are not imposed and we take a year or two to make decisions [involving the whole program]."

Key staff and administration also realize the need to continually assess the effectiveness of their program. Toward that end, adjustments and innovations are regularly discussed. The following are aspects of the program mentioned in statements made by program teachers, aides, and administrators with regard to the areas of the program that could be improved:

- More Spanish input needed (especially in Grades 1-2); more time and opportunities to use Spanish oral language for native English speakers.

- More Spanish language resource materials.

- Increased explicit language instruction (in meaningful contexts). [after the lessons on the past form of verbs] "They are more aware that that is one thing they need to say right; they're more conscientious about saying it right. . . . I'm going to do it next year because I see the progress, even though it's not perfect. But maybe as we get more organized and more structured, we'll see more progress."

- Homework support after school for students whose parents can't help them at home.
- More planning time for teachers. "What I would like to have is— I've been saying this— . . . 'Give us some more planning time—Give us some planning time. We don't have any.'" [What time is allocated is often taken up by meetings.]
- More second language acquisition training for teachers. "I'm firmly convinced that everybody in this program should have ESL background. . . . Isn't it better to know how language develops?"

Conclusions

This profile has described Francis Scott Key Elementary School's two-way immersion program after its eighth and ninth years of implementing a 50-50 program model. Key teachers use a number of strategies to support first and second language development, to negotiate meaning, and to provide high level instruction. Key's commitment to professional development has created a cadre of teachers trained in instructional strategies appropriate to the model. New and less inexperienced teachers at Key benefit from collaboration with their more experienced grade-level colleagues. The teachers and administrators are very supportive of the program and feel that it is having a very positive impact on the students' development of bilingualism and biliteracy, as well as on their academic achievement.

Looking at these results from the perspective of the students' English language proficiency, it is clear that the English-background students have not suffered at all in their continued development of English language arts, but rather have achieved high levels of performance. The results are even more dramatic for the native Spanish speakers. The Spanish-background students showed impressive gains in English language proficiency across the grades and were not only fluent, but largely indistinguishable from their native-English-speaking peers by fourth grade. Observations of selected students clearly showed that the Spanish-speaking students had acquired English and even preferred to use English in interactions with other English and Spanish speakers.

In addition, all of the Spanish-speaking students were fluent in Spanish, and the English speakers gained a high level of oral proficiency in Spanish across the grade levels. Classroom observations also demonstrated that, over the years, students build sufficient proficiency in Spanish to interact with the teacher and their peers during Spanish instruction. However, they showed a preference for speaking English and used English whenever they had the chance.

In summary, the objective that students would develop proficiency in two languages was met by both native English and native Spanish speakers, albeit to varying degrees. The students showed proficiency in all areas of development including pronunciation, vocabulary, grammar, and sociolinguistically appropriate use of the language. Academic performance goals were met as well. In content area skills, the 1995 ITBS scores show Key immersion students exceeding, on the average, their peers within the school, the district, and the state in all content areas tested. Overall, the administrators and teachers feel that the program is meeting its goals even as they continue working to improve it.

CHAPTER THREE
River Glen
Elementary School
San José (CA) Unified
School District

Program Information

Program Overview

The two-way bilingual immersion program at River Glen Elementary School in San José, California, provides an immersion model for native English speakers and a bilingual maintenance model for native Spanish speakers. The current program serves as a magnet school in the district. As of the 1994-1995 school year, River Glen included preschool through sixth grade and had 380 students.

River Glen's program follows the 90-10 two-way immersion model developed by the California State Department of Education (see section on *History* below). Table 3.1 shows the breakdown of language of instruction by grade level. In the 90-10 model at kindergarten and first grade, 90% of the instructional day is devoted to content instruction in Spanish and 10% to English. At the second and third grade levels, students receive 80-85% of their instruction in Spanish and 15-20% in English. By fourth and fifth grades, 60% of the instructional day is in Spanish and 40% in English. At the sixth grade level, the students' instructional time is evenly balanced between English and Spanish.

Table 3.1

90-10 Program Design by Grade Level at River Glen

Grade Level	% Instruction in Spanish	% Instruction in English
Kindergarten-First	90%	10%
Second	85%	15%
Third	80%	20%
Fourth-Fifth	60%	40%
Sixth	50%	50%

Program Goals

There are three major program goals at River Glen. The first is that students will become bilingual and biliterate by the end of seven years in the program. The second is that students will experience academic success by achieving at or above grade level in all subject areas. River Glen wants to ensure that all students are academically challenged and motivated to continue to study throughout their schooling career. The third goal is that students will acquire an appreciation and understanding of other cultures, while developing positive attitudes toward themselves and their academic abilities. An outgrowth of this goal is that students will develop a sense of advocacy for themselves and for children who speak other languages. (As noted in the introduction to this volume, this profile focuses primarily on the first two goals, but other sources (e.g., Lindholm, 1994) deal with the third.)

District and School Characteristics

The San José Unified School District is an urban school district located in Santa Clara County at the southern end of San Francisco Bay in northern California. San José Unified comprises 42 schools and has a total student enrollment of approximately 31,000. Table 3.2 presents the percentage of students from different ethnic groups, the percentage of students receiving free or reduced-price lunches, and the percentage of limited English proficient students in the district and at River Glen School.

In San José Unified's diverse district, Hispanic students make up 46% of the student body; 35% are European American, 14% Asian American, 4% African American, and 1% Native American. Approximately 25% are classified as limited English proficient (LEP), and 42% participate in the free/reduced-price lunch program.

Approximately 68% of the River Glen school's population is Hispanic, with 29% European American, 2% African American, 1% Asian American, and less than 1% (.3%) Native American. Over half (54%) of River Glen's students enter school with limited English proficiency. Although 47% of River Glen's students are from low-income households, only 16% of the native-English-speaking students participate in the free lunch program, whereas 75% of the native-Spanish-speaking students participate.

Table 3.2

District and School Characteristics: Percentage of Students from Different Ethnic Backgrounds, on the Free Lunch Program, and Limited English Proficient (1995)

	District (31,000 students)	School (380 students)
Ethnic Breakdown		
Hispanic	46%	68%
European American	35%	29%
African American	4%	2%
Asian American	14%	1%
Native American	1%	0%*
Free/Reduced-Price Lunch	42%	47%
LEP Population	25%	54%

*All figures are rounded. The population of Native Americans is .3%.

History

To assist in the San José Unified School District's desegregation efforts, River Glen's two-way bilingual immersion program was founded in 1986 as a magnet program within the communications magnet theme at Washington Elementary School. Conceived by the Office of Bilingual Education at the California State Department of Education in 1985 following the successful San Diego model, the proposed two-way bilingual immersion model combined the most salient features of a maintenance bilingual education model for language minority students with a foreign language immersion model for language majority students. The State Department of Education issued a request for interest to pilot the program, resulting in the selection of five school districts: San José, San Francisco, Oakland, Santa Monica/Malibu and San Diego. The five districts were to comprise a cooperative so that training, resources, and communication would be facilitated during program planning and implementation. That same year, the Office of Bilingual Education in Sacramento applied for a federal Title VII cooperative grant to help fund the bilingual immersion cooperative in the five identified districts. The grant was not awarded, but one year later, in 1986, the grant application was resubmitted and subsequently revised and approved for funding to implement two-way bilingual immersion programs in San José, San Francisco, and Oakland.

Also in 1986, the San José Unified School District came under court order to desegregate its schools. The district proposed a voluntary participation desegregation plan that was approved by the court and left the district under the supervision of a court-appointed Desegregation Compliance Monitor.

In order to receive desegregation funding, participating schools in the district needed to create a magnet program that would attract a range of diverse students from among the district's population. The two-way program was labeled an early foreign language instruction magnet program. In 1986, the program began with two kindergarten and one first grade classroom at Washington Elementary School. At this time, there were three distinct programs in operation at Washington Elementary: the English monolingual program for English speak rs, a transitional bilingual program for Spanish speakers, and the two-way program.

In 1987, the program received another Title VII grant, which allowed it to expand by one grade level per year. By 1989, the program's pace at Washington Elementary School was no longer sufficient. The program became a satellite of Washington School and was moved from its original site near downtown San José to the River Glen site in the largely middle-class and English-speaking Willow Glen neighborhood. Though the new site took the program out of the mostly Spanish-speaking community of Washington Elementary, native Spanish speakers' enrollment at River Glen wavered only slightly. For desegregation purposes, River Glen's enrollment was still considered part of Washington's student population, as the two schools continued a collaborative relationship. The River Glen campus also housed two community programs: the Alzheimer's Center and the Mexican-American Community Services Agency (MACSA).

By 1991, the two-way program had grown to include Grades K-6 and was serving 260 students. Both the Alzheimer's Center and MACSA had left the site, and the program was able to appropriate the office area and a portable classroom for its use. Also in 1991, the program applied for and received a three-year Title VII developmental bilingual education grant to support preschool and middle school expansion. Additionally, a Community Development Block Grant was approved by the City of San José to finance a preschool building whose construction was completed in December 1992. With the addition of this building and its component preschool program in January 1993, River Glen began providing services to a Spanish-speaking feeder population for its kindergarten. Mobile classrooms have been added to the site for the library/media center, and River Glen now provides extended day care for students before and after school.

The current principal came to River Glen in 1994. The former principal (from 1989 to 1994) is still at River Glen but currently focuses her efforts on a Title VII-funded academic excellence project to expand the two-way program to other schools around the country.

The two-way bilingual immersion program at River Glen has received two awards for academic excellence: (1) The Santa Clara

Glenn Hoffman Exemplary Program Award, 1989; and (2) The California Association for Bilingual Education's (CABE) Exemplary Bilingual Practices Award, 1991, for meeting the needs of language minority students. In addition, River Glen has been recognized by the California State Department of Education and the U.S. Department of Education's Office of Bilingual Education and Minority Languages Affairs (OBEMLA) as an Academic Excellence school and has received funding from OBEMLA to disseminate its two-way bilingual immersion model throughout the state and nation.

Program Features

Administrative Factors

River Glen has received mixed support from the San José Unified School District administration and Board of Education. Though its program has received laudatory attention around the country, River Glen parents and staff have had to work hard to gain district support and approval for the program. A few individual board members or administrators have been very supportive, but in general there has been little support from the administration or school board.

At the school-site level, there is exceptional leadership and support. The former principal and the current principal have considerable knowledge of the characteristics that make a school and a second language education program effective. They communicate high expectations for all students and assure that the staff, parents, and students live up to these expectations. They make certain that teachers are fully trained and observe them frequently in the classroom. They provide for follow-through in professional development, involve teachers in decision making, and discuss the curriculum at staff meetings with careful attention to articulation across grade levels.

Another source of administrative assistance is the extremely capable curriculum specialist. She has been with the program since it began at Washington School and understands the program model and how to implement it well. By considering the theoretical and pedagogical implications of any proposed changes, she has helped the program to improve. This careful attention to the theory and peda gogy underlying the model has helped River Glen become an exemplary 90-10 program.

Teachers and Staff

The six teachers observed at River Glen (Grades 1-6) came from Spanish, English, and bilingual backgrounds. All teachers were women; four were of Mexican or Latin American descent, and two were of European descent. All were bilingual. They have had social, linguistic, and educational experiences in Mexico, Guatemala, Colombia, China, and various states in the union. Although River Glen has no formal Spanish proficiency requirement for teachers who teach in Spanish, their language proficiency is assessed informally by an administrator during the hiring interview. All teachers had very high levels of Spanish and English proficiency, though the proficiency levels varied somewhat from teacher to teacher. Some teachers were native speakers of Spanish and had been educated in Spanish. Other teachers were bilingual from childhood or learned Spanish as adults. The multicultural background of the teachers showed in their pedagogy and blended well with the diverse elements that the students themselves brought to the classroom.

All six teachers maintained extremely positive attitudes toward the program and its staff and students. They believed the program to be very effective, helping to create high social and academic standards for leadership and learning among the students.

There was a high degree of teacher turnover just before and during the observation period. The limited experience and training of many of the teachers observed affected student interactions and outcomes. In the first year of the observation of this program, there were three teachers new to the program and new to teaching. Thus, the first grade teacher preferred not to be included in the observations. The fifth grade teacher left in December and a new Spanish-language teacher could not be located. As a result, the fifth graders spent more than half of the year studying largely in English. At the end of that year, another four teachers left the staff, so the second year of observations involved another new set of teachers. With so many new staff in a relatively short period, the program had to confront staff inexperience as an issue. It should be noted that the departing teachers did not leave because they were dissatisfied, but because they needed to relocate to a different area or stop working due to illness or maternity leave. Another teacher moved to a new school to assume an administrative position.

Curriculum

The instructional content at River Glen is equivalent to that for other students at the same grades in the San José Unified School District. However, since River Glen's program is a 90-10 immersion model, schedules are carefully structured to teach all required academic subjects using methods that are appropriate for both grade-level achievement and bilingual (Spanish/English) language acquisition.

Table 3.3 shows the content areas taught in each language at each grade level. In the 90-10 model at kindergarten and first grade, all content instruction occurs in Spanish, and English time is used to develop oral language proficiency. Reading instruction begins in Spanish for both Spanish-speaking and English-speaking students. At the second and third grade levels, when students receive 80-85% of their instruction in Spanish and 15-20% in English, all content is taught in Spanish. In second grade, English time is largely spent in developing oral language proficiency, but beginning to develop academic language skills in English. In third grade, students begin formal English reading. At the fourth-, fifth-, and sixth-grade levels, when students spend close to half their day in each language, the content areas taught in each language depend on the available curriculum materials and supporting resource materials. However, an attempt is made to assure that students are given opportunities to develop academic language in each of the major curricular areas.

The late introduction to formal English reading is an important part of the program model. The implementation of English reading instruction requires a requisite level of Spanish language literacy. When examining students' achievement test scores in English, it is important to keep in mind that students do not read in English until third grade.

Table 3.3

90-10 Curriculum Design by Language Grade Level

Grade Level	Science/ Health	Social Studies	Math	Language Arts
Kindergarten-First	Spanish	Spanish	Spanish	Spanish* and English
Second	Spanish	Spanish	Spanish	Spanish* and English
Third	Spanish	Spanish	Spanish	Spanish* and English
Fourth-Fifth	Spanish	English	Spanish	Spanish and English
Sixth	English	Spanish	Spanish	Spanish and English

* indicates the language of reading instruction

Professional Development

Professional development is a high priority at River Glen. Teachers receive extensive training and professional development in a number of areas. College courses and inservice workshops are the predominant means of teacher development in topics related to Spanish language, English language, linguistics, cross-cultural communication, cultural awareness, instructional methodology in Spanish and English, educational assessment, and educational research. All new teachers receive training in the theory and rationale for the two-way bilingual immersion model and in second language development. Then teachers are trained in cooperative learning, educational equity, and in effective instructional techniques appropriate to promoting achievement in language arts, mathematics, science, social studies, critical thinking, and technology. Training has also included how to articulate the issues across the grade levels and has integrated follow-through activities to ensure that the issues focused on during training are implemented in the classroom. At River Glen there is also a great deal of team teaching, idea-sharing, and self- and group-examination.

Parental Involvement

There is considerable parent involvement at the school. Parents volunteer their time as teaching assistants, recess and lunch monitors, facilitators for school tours, developers of program brochures, and speakers at workshops and conferences. In addition, parents have high attendance at home-school workshops, parent-teacher conferences, and other school-related activities.

A strong parent organization, called HABLA, is composed of both English- and Spanish-speaking parents. This organization functions to provide support to parents as well as parent support to the program. An important feature of HABLA is that it strongly endorses equal participation of all parents. Thus, all meetings are announced in both English and Spanish, and all presentations to the group and group meetings are completely bilingual (not merely translations from English into Spanish for a small group sitting in the corner). Because Spanish-speaking parents are encouraged to attend and made to feel welcome, their participation is very strong, and they have assumed strong leadership roles in home-school activities.

Learning Environment

Classroom

All of the classrooms observed had a variety of stimulating and colorful materials on bulletin boards and arranged around the classroom. Any language displayed in the classroom materials matched the language(s) taught in the room. Thus, if the teacher used only Spanish, then all materials were in Spanish, including all bulletin boards, posters, and books. For those teachers that split their instructional time between English and Spanish, there were bulletin boards, posters, and other instructional materials in the two languages and books in both languages as well. In all classes, students' work was displayed.

Teachers used cooperative group seating. The desks in each classroom were arranged in groups of three to six. In each seating group, the students sat at their desks side by side and facing one another.

Most announcements from the principal's office were made in Spanish. Assemblies were frequently conducted in English, however, unless there were Spanish-speaking presenters.

The teachers worked extensively with classroom aides and often split their class into two groups when an aide was in the room. If the aides were presenting the same material as the teacher, generally the class was split evenly. However, the aides also worked with smaller groups of students who required additional help on separate activities, while the teacher presented material to the rest of the class.

Library Resources

River Glen's library/media center contains reference and resource materials and books in both English and Spanish. There is a strong attempt to provide materials appropriate for each grade level in the appropriate language(s). However, at the upper grade levels, the students do not have much variety in interesting reading material in Spanish. More advanced books in Spanish of interest to the preteen group are difficult to locate. Thus, students turn to English book series such as the *Boxcar Children, Goosebumps, Nancy Drew,* and so on.

Technology Resources

Computers are used extensively in every classroom, with software available in both Spanish and English. Learning games and word processing were the most common applications observed, but some teachers also made combined use of the computer and overhead projector to present material and exercises. The library/media center provided large-screen television sets and VCRs for educational viewing. Some classrooms in the upper grades kept such equipment in the room at all times, while other classes requested it for a given time period.

Instructional Practices

Separation of Languages

Teachers adhered strictly to the language policy of the classroom. Because River Glen follows a 90-10 immersion model, each grade level had different language requirements (see Table 3.1), but the teachers never deviated from their individual language schedules. As a consequence, the students were required to listen, understand, and interact with the teacher in the appropriate language of the class. Until fifth grade, the students changed teachers when they received instruction in English. From fifth grade on—when the mix of English and Spanish language instruction was roughly equal—students remained with the same teacher and changed languages at certain points in the day and for different subjects.

Making Content Comprehensible

The teachers employed a number of means to make language and content comprehensible to the students. Most teachers used a variety of resources, such as the blackboard, overhead projectors, computers, videos, Venn diagrams, brainstorming, drama, and acting as well as concrete contextual references (visuals, realia) in their lessons.

Teachers at River Glen believe that their instructional strategies reflect good teaching. They use sheltering, student-teacher modeling, realia, Total Physical Response, illustrations, and rephrasing to improve comprehension and develop vocabulary. They believe that it is important to present material in a fashion that students can comprehend, and because learning styles and language needs vary among students, their presentation must also change to accommodate the students' needs. Most teachers also feel that content area instruction is influenced by a number of factors, one of which is the language needs of second language learners.

The teachers were very conscious of the need to provide comprehensible input and used a variety of question stems and ways of linking new vocabulary to previously learned material. Sheltering techniques were also employed, such as simplifying the language input when necessary; reviewing the main topic and key vocabulary; checking frequently for understanding; modifying their language to the needs of the students; and using rephrasing, paraphrasing, and synonyms. In many instances in the lower grades, the teachers had individual students or the entire class finish sentences for them. For example:

T: *y en nuestro jardín, podemos plantar una legumbre anaranjado que crece en la tierra, que llamamos . . .* (and in our garden, we can plant an orange vegetable that grows in the ground, that we call . . .)

Class: *¡zanahorias!* (carrots)

Teachers also monitored student comprehension through interactive means such as comprehension checks, clarification requests, a variety of questioning types, paraphrasing, providing definitions, expansion, scaffolding, and modeling. For example:

T: This week we're gonna be working on a collage.

Class: Collage?

T: Collage, a collage is a picture made up of a lot of different things; it can be words, it can be things, it can be objects. What I want you to do is to pick one of the main characters of Charlotte's Web and, to make it a little bit easier, we're gonna brainstorm and we're going to think of . . . (unintelligible). A brainstorm is where everybody gets a lot of ideas for your collage. But you're only gonna pick one—one that you wanna do. We'll do that one together and then maybe you'll get a better idea of what I want. Okay, we're gonna start with Charlotte. When you think of Charlotte in the story, what sort of things do you think about?

In the lower elementary classes, Total Physical Response (TPR) was frequently used by teachers to negotiate meaning with students. In addition to TPR and vocabulary checks, teachers across grade levels were very vigilant about their students' in-class work. When an assignment was given and work begun, every teacher walked around the class, checking student progress and offering assistance when needed. At times, the teacher needed only to walk about the room as the students worked silently. At other times, students raised their hands or formed lines waiting to discuss their work with the teacher. Whatever the case, the teacher did not resume the lesson until all students with a question had the opportunity to discuss their work with her.

Language Development Strategies

In Spanish, the teachers generally made use of the indicative, conditional, subjunctive, and imperative moods. Furthermore, most of the verb tenses were observed in the teachers' speech, including present and imperfect indicatives, preterit, future, conditional, present and imperfect subjunctive, imperative, and present perfect indicative. The more complicated compound tenses of preterit perfect or future perfect or past perfect subjunctive were observed infrequently. Teachers' language included conjunction and embedding.

The teachers believed they should not sacrifice content for language. Rather, they felt it was necessary to use challenging material to build the language skills of their students. These are some strategies recommended by the teachers:

• Promote a variety of activities and discussions that work to build vocabulary skills, which in turn influence the amount of information a student can take in.

• Model sophisticated language. Many teachers indicated that when a student obviously grasps the concept, but is having difficulty expressing that concept, they will reword or rephrase their utterances so that the student has a linguistic model to attach to the concept.

Teachers tended to correct student digressions from target language use more than they did actual linguistic errors. In the event of student linguistic errors, most teachers were likely either to let the error pass (if the utterance was intelligible) or simply model the appropriate form back to the student rather than inform the student that his or her use of the language was incorrect. Also, when students made an error, the teachers typically focused on the content as opposed to the structure of the student's response.

T: (asking the class for words that begin with the letter "y") *ok, ok, otro.* [another.] ¿Elena?

E: *¿llave?* [key?]

T: *ahh, llave.*

S1: *no, llave tiene doble ele.* [no, *llave* has two "l's".]

T: *pero tiene, pero Elena tiene razón que tiene, ¿qué?* [but she has, but Elena has a good reason to think that it has, what?]

S2: *dos ele.* [two "l's".]

T: *gracias . . . fantástico, Elena, que tú te fijaste que tiene sonidos casi iguales . . . muy bien . . . muy parecidos . . . muy parecidos.* [thank you . . . fantastic, Elena, that you noticed that they have almost equivalent sounds . . . very good . . . very similar ...very similar.]

Other Strategies

There was a strong emphasis on writing and creative exploration in the classroom, both in Spanish and English. Also, English and Spanish language instruction in the content areas was integrated and interrelated in the teachers' lesson plans and provided the students with a clear and well-conceived learning environment.

Student Grouping

Students experienced instruction in a number of different grouping contexts. During some portions of the day, they were engaged in whole class activities or individual seatwork. At other times, they worked in pairs. They also spent considerable time working in cooperative groups, and the physical layout of the classroom was designed around these groups. In each seating group, the students sat at their desks side by side and facing one another. The teachers changed the populations of each cooperative learning group as they saw fit throughout the year. Thus, students were moved to different groups a few times throughout the year. Each group reflected the population of the classroom, with fairly equal representations of ethnicity and English and Spanish speakers. Also, at the lower grades, teachers tried to assure that each group had a bilingual student who could translate if necessary.

Student Language Use

Separation of Languages

Across grade levels and in both academic and non-academic classroom situations, the speaking of English between students was frequently observed during Spanish time. At the upper grade levels, students were expected to speak Spanish during Spanish time, and teachers often requested students to use Spanish if they were using English. Students showed high levels of comprehension during classroom lecture, discussion, and work in both Spanish and English. When students at the upper grade levels were distanced from linguistic authority and given the opportunity to choose a language, more often than not they spoke English. There was some code-switching in student–student interactions. In the lower grades, students code-switched when they did not have the appropriate vocabulary or grammar in their second language. In the upper grades, however, the use of English during Spanish time did not reflect students' inability to express themselves fully in Spanish; using English was clearly a deliberate choice.

In the lower grades, students tended to be more consistent about speaking Spanish during Spanish time. Deviation from Spanish generally came in the form of intra-sentential code switching, though these students also switched inter-sententially.[9]

---

[9] *Inter*-sentential code switching indicates the change of language from one sentence to another (e.g., *Vamos a la biblioteca.* I need to get a couple of books.). *Intra*-sentential code switching refers to the change of language within a sentence (e.g., *Vamos a la* library. I need to get a couple of *libros*).

SEGMENT 1 (Student–Teacher Interaction)

S: *sí, y cuando hay mucha lluvia, pues tenemos* floods. [yes, and when there's a lot of rain, then we have floods.]

T: *sí, inundación.* [yes, floods]

S: *inundación.* [floods.]

SEGMENT 2 (Student–Teacher Interaction)

S: are these "takeaways?"

T: *sí, restar.* [yes, subtraction.]

SEGMENT 3 (Student–Student Interaction)

S1:   what's the *respuesta* [answer] . . . ok, so what's *resolver* [to solve]?

S2:   (reading from text) it's *noventa y seis menos dieciseis,* plus *dieciseis* . . . no, wait, thirty-six plus thirty-eight [ninety-six minus sixteen, plus sixteen . . . no, wait . . .]

S3:   no, it's sixty-one.

S1:   ok, how many *abejas* [bees] in the colony then?

Second Language Fluency and Accuracy

Throughout the grade levels, both the Spanish and English speakers maintained their native language fluency and gained greater accuracy in using various grammatical, vocabulary, sociolinguistic, and semantic components. The Spanish speakers who were learning English understood and produced fluent English with appropriate pronunciation, grammar, and vocabulary. Furthermore, they demonstrated an understanding of sociolinguistic rules during communication exchanges. The challenge for these students was in developing the higher level cognitive-academic language for literacy tasks that would provide the foundation for their content instruction in English.

Among English speakers learning Spanish at the early grade levels, there was clear acquisition of comprehension skills in the first few months of the program. These comprehension skills continued to develop throughout their participation in the program. These students also used appropriate pronunciation and simple vocabulary and grammar in Spanish, and they did so quite fluently. Although in the upper grade levels, students were clearly able to express themselves with greater ease, they demonstrated more limited grammatical constructions and vocabulary than one would expect of a native speaker at the same grade level. Almost all of these students were rated by their teachers as proficient[10] in Spanish at the appropriate grade level.

The students' interactions with each other were fluid, though sometimes unpredictable. At times they would provide linguistic guidance for each other, while at others they would make fun of accents or word choice.

SEGMENT 4

S1: *¿dónde está Juan?* [where is Juan?]

S2: *él, eh, ¿cómo se dice* "woke up late"? [he, uh, . . . how do you say "woke up late"?]

S1: *se despertó tarde.* [he woke up late.]

S2: *sí.* [yes.]

SEGMENT 5

T: *¿que encontrará?* [what will he find?]

S1: *un bote.* [a boat.]

S2: (nudges S1) *es un bote.* [it's a boat.]

S1: that's what I said, *un bote.*

S2: you said "*un botay.*" (emphasizes English accent)

S1: oh, just relax.

Whether or not these students were breaking rules or adhering to them, they were making consistent use of both Spanish and English. Although there seemed to be a disproportionate amount of English in their social language, the students were able to comprehend spoken and written Spanish and English and were able to produce meaningful, fluent speech in both languages.

---

[10] Students' proficiency was rated with respect to comprehension, fluency, pronunciation, grammar, and vocabulary (See Table 3.4 on page 65).

Student Written Work

Analyses of writing samples for selected individual students indicated that students were developing strong academic language skills in the upper grades. Because teachers had the students develop story webs and outlines, their written work tended to reflect this preliminary organization. Furthermore, there was evidence of appropriate sentence structure, spelling, punctuation, and verb tenses. In the few writing samples analyzed, students produced a few sentence embeddings and complex constructions. Students' writing reflected a variety of verb tenses and good subject-verb and adjective-noun agreement. Students also made the distinction between the use of *ser* and *estar*. (Both mean "to be" in English, but have distinctly different uses in Spanish.) The following portion of a writing sample was produced by a native-English-speaking fourth grader:

Empecé el cuarto grado en River Glen con la Maestra García. Yo no sabía que temas íbamos a aprender. Me dí cuenta que íbamos a estudiar California. Yo no sabía muchas cosas de California pero ahora sé bastante. La Misión Santa Clara es muy bonita. Queda muy cerca a San José. Es interesante aprender del estado en que uno vivo. Aprendí mucho de California porque hay mucho que aprender. . . . Ahora cuando mis padres quieren saber algo de California, piden información de mí. . . . Aprendí como Thomas Edison se pusó sordo cuando una persona jaló su oido. No sabía que una persona podía perder su sentido de oir.

[I started fourth grade at River Glen with Teacher Garcia. I didn't know what topics we would be learning. I found out that we were going to study California. I didn't know many things about California but now I know a lot. Santa Clara Mission is very pretty. It is located very close to San José. It is interesting to learn about the state in which one lives. I learned a lot about California because there is much to learn. . . . Now when my parents want to know something about California, they ask me. . . . I learned how Thomas Edison became deaf when a person pulled his ear. I didn't know that a person could lose their sense of hearing.]

Student Outcomes

Oral Language Development

Student outcomes regarding language proficiency were derived from the Student Oral Language Observation Matrix (SOLOM) and the Language Assessment Scales (LAS).

Table 3.4 presents the average ratings of first through fifth grade students on the Spanish SOLOM administered by teachers at the end of the year. Across grade levels, the Spanish SOLOM scores were very high for Spanish speakers, with average scores of 23.8-24.7 (out of a possible score of 25). For English speakers, scores generally increased across the grade levels. By first grade, at least half of the English speakers were rated fluent in Spanish, and by fourth grade, almost all of them were.

Table 3.5 shows corresponding LAS scores for the English oral proficiency of Spanish speakers. Among native Spanish speakers, the percentage of students designated as fluent in English (Levels 4 and 5) increased from 50% in Grade 1 to 74% in Grade 2, 95% in Grade 3, and 100% in Grades 4 through 6. Average scores increased from 62 in Grade 1 to 87 in Grade 6.

In sum, results from the LAS and the SOLOM were consistent in showing that the English-speaking students were making progress in Spanish oral language skills and were maintaining their high oral language proficiency in English. Spanish-speakers continued to advance in Spanish while making impressive gains in oral English language proficiency. By third grade, the majority of Spanish-speaking students scored as fluent English proficient and a majority of the English-speaking students scored as fluent Spanish proficient.

Table 3.4

Spanish SOLOM: Average Score and Percentage of Students Scoring Fluent by Grade Level and Language Background (1995)

Grade Level and Language Background	Percent Fluent	Average Score
First Grade:		
Spanish Speakers	100%	24.7
English Speakers	60%	21.6
Second Grade:		
Spanish Speakers	100%	24.7
English Speakers	47%	18.4
Third Grade:		
Spanish Speakers	100%	24.4
English Speakers	77%	19.5
Fourth Grade:		
Spanish Speakers	100%	23.8
English Speakers	95%	22.2
Fifth Grade:		
Spanish Speakers	100%	24.2
English Speakers	100%	23.7

Table 3.5

English LAS: Average Score and Percentage of Spanish-Speaking Students Scoring Fluent (1995)

Grade Level	Percent Fluent	Average Score
First Grade	50%	62
Second Grade	74%	73
Third Grade	95%	79
Fourth Grade	100%	80
Fifth Grade	100%	91
Sixth Grade	100%	87

Academic Achievement

Reading and Writing Achievement in Spanish. The goal at River Glen is for students to perform at or above grade level in Spanish reading and writing. Table 3.6 shows the students' average percentiles from the *La Prueba Riverside de Realización en Español* reading and writing achievement subtests for each grade level (first through sixth). Attention to Table 3.6 indicates that performance in the first through sixth grades was at or above average (average defined as performance at the 50th percentile) in reading, with percentiles between 49 and 75. Writing achievement was also above average, with percentiles ranging from 60 to 69.

Mathematics, Social Studies, and Science Achievement in Spanish. Table 3.7 presents the percentiles from the *La Prueba* achievement test in the areas of mathematics, social studies, and science. Attention to Table 3.7 indicates that mathematics, social studies, and science performance was average to high for all grades, with percentiles for the grade levels between 54 and 76.

Table 3.6

Spanish Reading and Writing Achievement Scores in Percentiles (1995)

Grade Level	Reading Achievement in Percentiles	Writing Achievement in Percentiles
First Grade	75	—
Second Grade	49	—
Third Grade	54	69
Fourth Grade	60	68
Fifth Grade	50	69
Sixth Grade	57	60

Table 3.7

Spanish Mathematics, Social Studies, and Science Achievement Scores in Percentiles (1995)

Grade Level	Mathematics Achievement in Percentiles	Writing Achievement in Percentiles	Science Achievement in Percentiles
First Grade	69		
Second Grade	60		
Third Grade	68	69	68
Fourth Grade	72	67	69
Fifth Grade	59	76	58
Sixth Grade	61	54	64

Reading and Language Achievement in English. Table 3.8 shows the students' average percentiles from the *Comprehensive Test of Basic Skills* (CTBS) reading and language achievement subtests. (It is important to remember that students did not begin reading instruction in English until third grade.) Attention to Table 3.8 indicates that the average percentiles for all students increased across grade levels in both reading and language: in reading from the 34th percentile in third grade to the 51st percentile in seventh grade, and in language from the 27th percentile in third grade to the 52nd percentile in seventh grade.

Table 3.8

English Reading and Language Achievement Scores in Percentiles by Grade Level (1995)

Grade Level	Reading Achievement in Percentiles	Language Achievement in Percentiles
Third Grade	34	27
Fourth Grade	44	52
Fifth Grade	37	43
Sixth Grade	32	40
Seventh Grade	51	52

Mathematics Achievement in English. Attention to Table 3.9 indicates that the average percentiles in English mathematics increased from below average in third grade (47th percentile) to above average in seventh grade (63rd percentile), with decrements in fifth and sixth grades.

Table 3.9

English Mathematics Achievement Scores in Percentiles (1995)

Grade Level	Mathematics Achievement in Percentiles
Third Grade	47
Fourth Grade	54
Fifth Grade	36
Sixth Grade	37
Seventh Grade	63

Program Impact

River Glen's teachers and principal were very optimistic about the impact that participation in the program was having and will continue to have on the students. Overall, they believed that the ethnic and linguistic diversity of River Glen helped students to establish a healthy and realistic world view. Teachers said that in both working and interpersonal relationships, the cognitively demanding nature of River Glen's curriculum helps the students to break down the barriers that pose so many problems in the United States today. The teachers also maintained that students learn to be leaders by participating in this program. Since River Glen receives a great deal of recognition for its innovative and successful approach to teaching, students gain a sense of pride, confidence, and enthusiasm. Teachers noted that, for the most part, students understand the importance of their bilingualism in both a macro/societal and micro/individual context.

All teachers interviewed agreed that River Glen is a successful two-way bilingual immersion program. These are some aspects of the program that teachers felt were working particularly well:

* Well-defined two-way bilingual immersion model
* Thematically integrated curriculum
* Cross-grade articulation

- Commitment to self-examination and evaluation
- Team teaching
- Strong sense of respect between teachers and students
- Parental involvement
- School-home newsletter

Teachers identified the following items as important to make the program more effective:
- ESL/vocabulary development of LEP students
- Spanish-language resource materials
- Spanish-language assemblies
- More qualified and experienced bilingual professionals for the upper grades

Conclusions

This chapter presents a profile of River Glen Elementary School after its eighth year of implementing the 90-10 two-way bilingual immersion model. River Glen administrators and teachers have worked hard to define and adhere carefully to the model at their school site. Teachers use a number of strategies to support first and second language development, to negotiate meaning, and to provide high level instruction. Because of River Glen's commitment to professional development, teachers have been trained to understand clearly the two-way model and to implement appropriate instructional strategies important to the model. However, because there were two years of high teacher turnover and thus the hiring of new and inexperienced teachers at River Glen during the period this program was examined, the observations and student outcomes are not as positive as they had been in previous years. But the teachers and administrators are very supportive of the program and feel that it is having a very positive impact on the students' development of bilingualism and biliteracy.

Looking at these results from the perspective of the students' English language proficiency, it is clear that the English-speaking students were fully proficient, as expected. The results are even more dramatic for the Spanish speakers. In spite of the limited instructional time in English, the Spanish speakers showed growth in English language proficiency across the grades, with all but one of the native Spanish-speaking third through fifth graders scoring as fluent English proficient. Observations of selected students clearly showed that the Spanish-speaking students had acquired English and even preferred to use English in interactions with other English and Spanish speakers.

In addition, all of the Spanish-speaking students were fluent in Spanish, and the English speakers made great gains in Spanish oral language proficiency across the grade levels. By the third grade level, all but one of the English speakers were rated as fluent Spanish proficient. Classroom observations also demonstrated that students had the proficiency in Spanish to interact with the teacher during Spanish instruction. However, students showed a preference for speaking English and engaged in English whenever they had the chance.

Thus, the objective that students become proficient in two languages was clearly met by both native English and native Spanish speakers. The students showed proficiency in all areas of development including pronunciation, vocabulary, grammar, and sociolinguistically appropriate use of the language.

The majority of the English and Spanish speakers performed well on the achievement test in Spanish, scoring average to high. Their above-grade-level scores in reading and mathematics demonstrate that they were developing appropriate reading comprehension, vocabulary and study skills, writing skills, mathematics computation and problem solving skills, and social studies and science concepts.

English achievement varied considerably, as expected (taking into account that students did not begin English reading instruction until third grade). Scores prior to third grade represent transfer from Spanish reading instruction and perhaps parental or other extracurricular help (e.g., *Sesame Street*, older siblings or peers) in English reading. It is important to keep in mind that students who do not begin English reading instruction until third grade have to make significant gains each year to catch up statistically to their peers who began English reading two years earlier and who continue to develop their English skills.

Performance in English reading increased steadily across the grade levels and reached the 50th percentile by seventh grade. However, English speakers scored at or above the 50th percentile from third grade on. Thus, while students scored very well in Spanish reading and had been fluent in communicative exchanges in English for three years, as a group, they were still scoring only average in the decontextualized area of language arts/reading. In contrast, students scored average to above average in English mathematics, with seventh graders scoring at the 63rd percentile.

In conclusion, the results of our study are positive and demonstrate that the English and Spanish speakers are becoming bilingual and biliterate, with average to high levels of content area knowledge. The administrators and teachers at River Glen are all very satisfied with the program and the way students are learning.

CHAPTER FOUR
Inter-American Magnet School Chicago (IL) Public Schools

Program Information

Program Overview

Inter-American Magnet School (IAMS) is a pre-kindergarten through eighth grade school located in one of Chicago's northside neighborhoods. IAMS is a two-way immersion school; that is, all students in the school participate in the *dual language program*.[11] About half of the students enrolled in the school are Spanish dominant, and the other half are English dominant. Parents apply to send their children to IAMS. Because of the school's popularity, there is a waiting list. A computer lottery selects applicants from throughout the city in order to keep an ethnic and gender balance. Siblings of current students are given preference for admission, and a few slots are reserved each year for special cases, such as children of IAMS faculty.

The dual language program at IAMS, which follows the 80-20 model, benefits from effective leadership and administration, a capable bilingual teaching and support staff, and active parent and community support. The principal functions as the leader of the instructional team but shares decision-making authority with the Local

---

[11] This is how the Chicago Public Schools refer to their two-way immersion programs; their term will be used in this chapter.

School Council, which is an elected group of parents, teachers, and community members. The instructional team consists of teachers, tutors, aides, and classroom volunteers. The program also has a full-time Program Coordinator/Curriculum Developer, who serves as a resource on curriculum, disseminates information to other schools, provides in-service training opportunities, oversees the budget and purchasing, and coordinates visits by observers.

Table 4.1

80-20 Program Design by Grade Level at IAMS

Grade Level	Percentage of Instruction in Spanish	Percentage of Instruction in English
K-Third	80	20
Fourth-Fifth	60	40
Sixth-Eighth	50	50

The primary goal of IAMS is for students to become bilingual and biliterate while mastering academic content. The school is committed to a developmental bilingual education model based upon the following beliefs:

1) Fluency and literacy in English and Spanish are assets.

2) The best time to learn a second language is as early in life as possible.

3) Given appropriate exposure and motivation, children can learn another language.

4) Given appropriate instruction and the necessary home/school support, all children can achieve their fullest potential in all areas of the curriculum.

5) Caring, accepting, and cooperative behavior on the part of school staff, parents, and students promotes the development of the whole child.

District and School Characteristics

The Chicago Public School District consists of 473 elementary schools and 78 secondary schools with 412,000 students. Minority students make up 88% of the total student population. Chicago has 55% of Illinois's low-income students, 58% of its LEP students, and approximately 20% of the state's students with disabilities.

Now 20 years old and one of the oldest two-way immersion programs in the country, IAMS is the oldest of Chicago's 10 developmental bilingual (dual language immersion) programs. The school is located in a northside neighborhood in Chicago. It is housed in an aging yet sturdy three-story building. The school's playground and basketball courts lie between the street and the school's entrance, across from a row of somewhat older single-family and multiple-family houses. Inside the school, the hallway displays of student projects, such as *Los Grandes Reyes de Africa* (The Great Kings of Africa) and "African Proverbs," reflect the bilingual environment and the school's emphasis on multicultural education.

The school's total enrollment in 1994 was 621 students. Of these, 34.5% were limited English proficient (LEP). In addition, about 45% of the students entered the program already bilingual. Almost 60% of the students came from low-income households. There were 44 students identified as learning disabled (LD) who were partially included in the mainstream classes, but who also received pull-out support from one part-time and two full-time LD teachers. The student body was 71% Hispanic, 14.7% European American, 12.6% African American, and 1.2% either Asian/Pacific Islander or Native American.

The school's attendance rate (94.6%) was higher than the district's (88.7%) and the state's (93.2%). Its student mobility rate (8.5%) was substantially lower than both the district's and the state's, as was the school's average class size.

Table 4.2

District and School Characteristics: Percentage of Students from Different Ethnic Backgrounds, on Free Lunch Program, and Limited English Proficient (1994)*

	District (412,000 students)	School (600 students)
Ethnic Breakdown		
Hispanic	30%	71%
European American	12%	15%
African American	56%	13%
Asian American	3%	1%
Native American	0	0
Free/Reduced-Price Lunch	79%	60%
LEP Population	14%	35%

*All figures are rounded.

History

In a sense, one could say that Inter-American's dual language program is a family affair. Twenty years ago, the program was born of two parent/teachers' desire to see their children in a classroom where English-and Spanish-speaking children would be together, learning each other's language and culture. Originally, just a pre-school was planned, but the next year the program was continued into kindergarten. The parents and teachers then pushed district officials to increase the program grade by grade annually to third grade. At that point, the program contemplated freezing and remaining a PK-3 program, because it had completely taken over the school it had been placed in. Instead, it was decided to expand the program to a school-within-a-school in a larger building. The program was independent there and expanded into fourth and fifth grade. The program remained at that site for about three years, but it again outgrew the space available. At this point, the district superintendent offered the program the chance to move into one of several schools that were being underutilized. Principals of these candidate schools, however, were not eager to take the program, because the parents and teachers involved were very specific and insistent about how they wanted their program implemented. Finally, in 1983, a school was persuaded to accept the program, which would now include sixth grade. The district superintendent, who was very supportive of the dual language approach, announced on the radio that Inter-American would be a prototype program for other bilingual programs in the city.

In 1983, it was decided that three new schools that were being started with federal desegregation funds would be dual language schools. Many of the IAMS program staff left to help start one of the schools, Sabin Elementary. This was the same year that the IAMS program moved to the building where it is presently housed. It had to absorb 280 students who were already attending the school. The 280 students were offered the choice of entering the dual language program or moving to another school. Most of them stayed. It was a difficult year for a variety of reasons. The principal was not used to strong parent involvement and teacher participation in decision making. Some of the teachers who had already been at the school were very negative toward the program. Concerned parents and experienced dual language teachers began to complain that the principal was not very supportive of the program. Eventually, parents of the program began attending school board meetings to protest against the principal. Shortly thereafter, in 1985, the principal took early retirement.

A school committee then chose the current principal. The committee had wanted to hire a person who spoke Spanish. The woman who got the job, however, was an immigrant from Hungary who had lived in Nazi Germany. Upon arriving in this country at the age of 13, she was placed in first grade because she couldn't speak English. Her background, the committee felt, gave this woman the sensitivities to the reality faced by linguistically and culturally diverse students that they were looking for in a candidate. The current principal is also multilingual. In addition to her native Hungarian, she speaks German, flawless English, and in the last 10 years has managed to learn Spanish, using it whenever possible in the school. Since her arrival, the program has undergone continual development and modification.

In 1989, one of the founding parent/teachers took a position in the district bilingual education office. Her experience with Inter-American led her to promote the dual immersion model at the district level. In 1990, the district was awarded a Title VII grant to establish seven dual immersion programs. The founding parent/teacher was named Title VII project manager of the Chicago Public Schools' dual language immersion programs. Under her direction, staff development and training modules were developed and implemented in a standardized way throughout the district.

In recent years, other bilingual programs in the district have begun to pattern themselves after the IAMS dual language model. With a strong model at IAMS and support from the district's bilingual education office, these programs are gradually overcoming fears that their students would not be able to function academically in such a program. Chicago's dual language programs have now expanded to 10 schools, educating over 3,100 children. At IAMS, the other founding parent/teacher continues to teach. A former dual language student is currently student teaching at IAMS, and grandchildren of IAMS teachers are now attending the school. The school even grants a scholarship each year to one graduating senior who decides to go to college. The student receives $500 for each year he or she stays in college. The family affair continues.

As mentioned above, the district has been very supportive of the dual language approach to bilingual education. Its confidence in such programs is reflected in the expansion of dual language to 10 schools.

The community continues to be very supportive of IAMS. Community members play an active role in such governing and ancillary bodies as the Local School Council and the Bilingual Advisory Committee (see below). Through these channels, the community, in cooperation with the administration and staff, identifies priorities and helps guide the school's instructional and extracurricular activities.

Program Features

Administrative Features

As mandated by Illinois state educational reform laws, the Local School Council (LSC) is the governing body of the school. It has 11 members: the principal, two teachers, two community representatives, and six parents. The LSC is responsible for choosing and retaining a principal; setting the course of the school improvement plan; establishing the priorities, procedures, and objectives for the school; and controlling discretionary funds. Chapter 1 discretionary funds from the state have been used in recent years to pay the salaries of five teachers and two instructional aides, which has helped lower class sizes (under 22 students on the average).

Within the school, the dual immersion program benefits from having a full-time program coordinator who carries out a wide range of activities. She works on the budget and financing, occasionally writing grant proposals to fund special projects or staff positions. She conducts inservice training for teachers from IAMS and the Chicago Public Schools and disseminates information about two-way immersion in general and IAMS's program in particular to all interested. On the instructional level, she assists teachers in selecting texts and planning and developing curricula. She is also involved in administering some standardized tests (e.g., *La Prueba*).

In accordance with the familial nature of IAMS, it is felt that students can and should play a role in deciding issues of school governance and procedure that directly affect them. Recently, students contributed to decisions to extend the school day and recess period and to establish a dress code. Students also participated in the most recent evaluation of the principal.

Teachers and Staff

The faculty at IAMS reflects the balance between Spanish and English and the equal status the two languages hold at the school. With the exception of the computer arts instructor and the librarian, all 40 teachers at IAMS in 1995 were bilingual. Many were native

Spanish speakers from a variety of countries (e.g., Mexico, Cuba), and others were native English speakers who had either lived in Spanish-speaking countries, were raised bilingual, or had learned Spanish well enough to teach in it. Most members of the faculty held Master's degrees or had engaged in other postgraduate studies.

Teachers at IAMS were not only expected to be bilingual, they needed to believe in the dual language immersion approach and implement research-based instruction in their classrooms. The principal expected and encouraged the school's 40 teachers to be innovative in their pedagogy. She also encouraged them to create and maintain a positive affective environment in the school.

Along these lines, two further characteristics that may partially explain the success of IAMS were identified as *caring* and *daring*. Teachers, staff, students, and parents all worked together to create a safe and caring environment. Teachers knew students by name and treated the students as if they were family. Caring, however, was not enough to ensure academic success. The faculty used a sort of "tough love," daring students to learn and pushing them to do the work they needed to do to be successful.

These factors have contributed to the success of outstanding teachers at IAMS. Among these, one was chosen 1994 Illinois Teacher of the Year, and two others received the 1991 and 1994 Golden Apple Awards for Excellence in Teaching from the Golden Apple Foundation (Chicago).

Curriculum

Pre-kindergarten instruction is almost entirely in Spanish. From kindergarten to Grade 3, 80% of instructional time is in Spanish and 20% is in English. Students in the program learn to read in their native language and are therefore separated by language dominance for language arts classes until Grade 3. During these years, native English speakers work primarily through the oral language medium and are encouraged, but not required, to read and write in Spanish to the extent that they are able. (These students develop English reading and writing during their native language arts instruction and in many cases transfer those skills and begin reading in Spanish on their own.)

The program provides Spanish-dominant students with instruction in English as a second language (ESL) and English-dominant students with Spanish as a second language (SSL) on a daily basis.

From Grades 4-6, the language distribution ratio changes to 60-40 Spanish-English, and in Grades 7-8, it evens out at 50-50. During these years, students are fully integrated with regard to race, language dominance, and ability. Students from both language backgrounds, then, not only learn content together but also receive instruction in English language arts and Spanish language arts together. Students who need additional support in their second language—including newcomers to the program—may continue to receive separate instruction in ESL or SSL for as long as necessary.

The dual language program at IAMS originally followed a 50-50 model at all grade levels. In 1990, the school decided that the students were not achieving sufficiently high levels of proficiency in Spanish. Consequently, more instructional time in Spanish was added from pre-K to Grade 3. (See Table 4.3.) As a result, teachers and administrators have noted an improvement in Spanish proficiency levels without a corresponding drop in English proficiency levels. In 1996, the program extended the 80-20 distribution to fourth grade, and, according to the program coordinator and principal, may further extend it to fifth grade.

Since all IAMS teachers are bilingual, they all teach part of each day in each language. Students change classrooms and teachers for ESL, SSL, and native language arts, as well as for other classes, such as art, library, and computers. Some courses are offered in both languages; these are either taught by two teachers (e.g., traditional social studies in English and studies of the Americas in Spanish) or by one teacher who alternates units (e.g., one math unit in Spanish, the next in English).

Table 4.3

80-20 Curriculum Design by Language, Subject, and Grade Level

Grades/ Subjects	Science/ Health	Social Studies	Math	Language Arts
Grades 1-3	Spanish	Spanish	Spanish	Spanish and English
Grades 4-5	Spanish and English	Spanish and English	Spanish and English	Spanish and English
Grade 6	Spanish and English	Spanish and English	Spanish and English	Spanish and English

Native English Speakers: English

In addition to its emphasis on developing bilingual and biliterate students, the program incorporates a focus on technology and scientific advances of society. The bilingual curriculum follows the scope and sequence of the Chicago Public Schools and attempts to integrate into all subject areas the history, contributions, and cultures of the peoples of the Americas.

Professional Development

Teachers are in charge of their own professional development at IAMS. The teachers determine their own needs and the best way to address them. Once a week the teachers meet with the principal, during which time they may discuss areas in which they feel they need more training or instruction.

All new teachers are paired with an experienced teacher who serves as a mentor for their first year. For an initial period of time, the two meet once a week for 30-40 minutes, and less frequently thereafter. These sessions are meant to provide new faculty members with an understanding of the school's philosophy, classroom management procedures, curriculum integration, and administrative matters. Additionally, all teachers are given a teacher manual, which outlines the school's philosophy and goals, describes administrative procedures, and provides recommendations for "best practices" in the teaching of each major subject area (e.g., science, math, reading).

Teacher Cooperation and Teaming

IAMS teachers are divided into teams according to "cycles." These cycles include pre-primary (pre-K, K), primary (1, 2), middle (3, 4), intermediate (5, 6), and upper (7, 8). The teachers are also encouraged to collaborate with their colleagues at each grade level. Teachers within each cycle meet regularly to discuss curriculum and instructional strategies to provide the best program for the students. Teachers also work with parents, parent volunteers, student-teachers from nearby universities, and instructional aides.

IAMS faculty are also actively involved in development and modification of the overall program. Teachers collaborate on the development, planning, and implementation of the curriculum, as well as on examination and review of the program as a whole. They have been instrumental in bringing about such changes as lower class size, longer school days, alternative assessment, and a stronger Spanish immersion component.

Parental Involvement

Parents and community have an integral role in the dual language program. A Bilingual Advisory Committee consists of teachers, parents of limited English proficient (LEP) students, and community members. This committee consults with the principal and the Local School Council on issues that affect the program.

The Parent Advisory Committee (PAC) is a voluntary organization of parents that represents parental interests to the school and to the LSC. IAMS parents have traditionally been very active participants in school affairs. Through the PAC, parents contribute to school decision-making, support volunteer activity, and engage in fundraising. A Parent Volunteer Coordinator maintains a desk in the faculty resource room and assists teachers and students with diverse tasks such as commissioning student artwork for the school yearbook and ordering supplies for the staff photocopier.

Learning Environment

Classroom

Classrooms at IAMS are large and well lit. Desks are typically in groups of four. Displays are in Spanish and English and, in the lower grades, include the alphabet in both languages. There are also calendars and manipulatives for numbers and words. In the upper grades there are wall maps. Most classrooms have bookshelves stocked with English and Spanish books, although more are in English. Bilingual books are rarer. Strung throughout the classrooms and the hallways are paper linked chains with names of books that each student has read. This is part of a schoolwide program called Literacy Links/ *Enlaces de Lectura* meant to promote reading at all grade levels and award classes that read the most books.

Library Resources

The library contains primarily books in English, although the subject area category labels posted above the stacks are written in Spanish and English. There are encyclopedias and other reference materials in Spanish and a small section of Spanish-language fiction.

Technology Resources

The emphasis placed on education in technology is evident in the classrooms at IAMS. Most classrooms have one or two computers in the back of the room, which students use for a variety of purposes.

Many of the classrooms are also equipped with television sets and VCRs. Many have overhead projectors as well.

IAMS's computer lab, which is staffed by a full-time computer arts teacher, contains approximately 20 Macintosh and Windows-based computers. In addition to the computer arts teacher, a professor from DeVry Institute comes in periodically to help students write programs, and eighth graders have written programs in Spanish for younger students.

Educational software is available in English and Spanish, but not all of the software has equivalents in the other language. For example, there is ESL software (*The Rosetta Stone*, by Fairfield Language Technologies, which is an interactive, multimedia CD-ROM program) and SSL software (which basically reviews Spanish grammar through drills and exercises). Reading comprehension software is available in both languages, as is word processing (Macintosh's *Bilingual Writing Center*). The students use *Grolier's Interactive Encyclopedia* on CD-ROM as a reference tool for other subject area projects.

Instructional Practices

Separation of Languages

While each class at IAMS is to be taught in one particular language, our observations revealed that teachers were not as exclusive in their use of that language during the instructional period as were teachers at the other two schools profiled. Teachers occasionally switched between languages during class time, providing instruction in English, for example, or admonishing a student in Spanish. When teachers felt the students did not completely understand a concept or certain instructions, translations were occasionally made. Some teachers also engaged in code-switching. For example, one third grade teacher taught in English but called on students using Spanish terms of endearment such as *mi hijo* (my son) or *mi hija* (my daughter). In interviews, teachers expressed strong aversion to consecutive translation as a model for making content comprehensible, because they believed it was not conducive to developing second language abilities.

Making Content Comprehensible

IAMS teachers used a variety of instructional strategies aimed at making content and language comprehensible and negotiating meaning with the students. Instructional tools, such as the computer, visuals (e.g., in Big Books, drawings on board), and graphic organizers were used frequently. In the lower grades, activities such as Total Physical Response, games, and use of manipulatives were employed. In terms of language usage, some teachers spoke slowly and clearly at all times, while others spoke at a normal pace and slowed down when they felt it was necessary. Verbal techniques, such as modeling language, sounding out words, defining, repeating, and rephrasing, along with nonverbal devices like miming, were used to facilitate comprehension. In the upper grades, student-centered activities such as cooperative learning and connecting to previous knowledge were utilized heavily. In general, the student-centered environment at IAMS allowed students to feel free to ask questions and make comments, permitting them to both fine-tune their understanding and practice using newly learned language and content.

Language Development Strategies

IAMS instruction is expected to be informed by current research in language acquisition and bilingual education. It was clear that teachers were attuned to the language needs of their students. A general set of instructional strategies believed to contribute to second language learning was used across grade levels at IAMS. These included the use of thematic instruction, cooperative learning, whole language, sheltered instruction, hands-on math and science, and reading and writing workshops.

Teachers at all levels appeared to monitor student comprehension regularly and allowed adequate time for students to produce utterances in the target language. In general, student errors in spoken language were not explicitly corrected by the teachers. The latter often modeled the correct word, word order, or form. In interviews, the teachers reported that modeling was their preferred form of error correction. In the one fifth grade SSL class observed, however, explicit correction of spoken errors was observed; and in a first grade classroom, written work was reviewed in class and feedback was provided, sometimes in the form of reminders such as *¡Las oraciones empiezan con mayúsculas!* (Sentences begin with capital letters!).

Student Language Use

In 1994-1995, approximately two thirds of IAMS students were Hispanic. About 45% of them entered the program bilingual; others knew only English, while still others knew only Spanish. State desegregation laws require that the percentage of language majority students not drop below 15%; thus, as a result of attrition it may become necessary to add monolingual English students to the program from the waiting list. The school will do this as late as fifth grade. While late-entry limited English proficient students receive additional one-on-one or small group ESL support, late-entry monolingual English-speaking students do not receive any Spanish support other than attending the same Spanish as a second language (SSL) classes as native English speakers who have been in the program since kindergarten. This presents a problem for teachers who teach in Spanish to these students, but program funds have not been able to cover the hiring of a teacher to provide additional Spanish support and tutoring.

Separation of Languages

It was clear that the language of preference among students was English. While some native Spanish speakers spoke in small groups in Spanish, most of the student utterances that were heard in and out of the classroom were in English. The teachers at IAMS generally tended to tolerate more English during Spanish time in the classroom than teachers in the other two programs observed. Some became less tolerant when the students directed their utterance to the teachers in English rather than Spanish. Teachers generally provided sufficient wait time for a student to formulate an utterance. If the student proved unable to do so in the language of instruction, however, teachers accepted student responses in the student's native language.

During instructional time in English, the students used only English. During instructional time in Spanish, students attempted to speak in Spanish to the extent they could when addressing the teacher.

As at the other two sites, English was clearly the preferred language for social purposes for those students who had achieved a certain level of fluency in it. At IAMS there appeared to be an even greater use of English by students when speaking among themselves than at the other two sites. Spanish, however, was often used socially by younger students or by more recent immigrants.

Teachers varied individually as to how much and by what means they reminded students to speak in the target language during a designated instructional period. Some teachers seemed to ignore student-to-student speech in English during Spanish time, while others occasionally shouted out reminders to speak in Spanish. In one instance observed, when a student was speaking in Spanish during English time, the teacher reminded, "Hey, English!" When the student continued in Spanish, the teacher simply said, "I don't understand you," and the student switched immediately to English.

If the students did not rigidly adhere to the separation of languages in the classroom, they expected the teacher to do so from early on, at least in the lower grades. Evidence of this was observed in one first grade classroom when the teacher was reading a story in English but pronounced the word *mango* as it would be in Spanish. At this point a student shouted, "Teacher, Spanish!" The teacher obediently reiterated the word using the English pronunciation.

Second Language Fluency and Accuracy

Since many of the students were bilingual when they entered the program, the level of English proficiency was rather high among the native Spanish speakers. Some errors were evident in early grades but appeared to work themselves out in subsequent years. In particular, errors observed in spoken English among first graders related to subject-verb inversion in embedded questions (e.g., "I know what is the treasure") and subject-verb agreement (e.g., "Yes, it do").

Getting the Spanish proficiency of both language groups to meet the English proficiency levels has been a challenge. While some English-dominant students excelled in Spanish, many did not see the need to learn Spanish (at least in the earlier grades) and were not motivated to learn it. The Spanish-dominant students, too, were so drawn by the dominance of English in society that they were not motivated to improve their Spanish language skills beyond oral proficiency. The program was working with the district bilingual office to determine what the high school standards for Spanish language classes were so that the program could work to prepare the students better to enter higher level Spanish courses (e.g., Spanish 2 or higher) in ninth grade.

Student Outcomes

Language Development

IAMS did not administer oral proficiency assessments but did assess reading and writing in Spanish. (English reading will be considered in the next section.) Table 4.4 shows students' average percentiles on a national scale from *La Prueba Riverside de Realización en Español* reading and writing subtests in Spanish. According to the scores, student achievement percentiles were average to above average. In 1995, students in the earlier grades, who receive more instruction in Spanish, seemed to be doing better than older students, who gradually receive less Spanish instruction.[12] (Note: IAMS did not separate its students by language background in reporting test scores.)

Table 4.4

Spanish Reading and Writing Achievement Scores in Percentiles at each Grade Level (1995)

Grade	Reading Achievement in Percentiles	Writing Achievement in Percentiles
3	69.1	67.0
4	64.5	70.0
5	60.6	62.2
6	61.3	53.2
7	58.9	66.8
8	61.9	57.0

[12] In addition, it should be kept in mind that students in Grades 6-8 in 1995 began the program when the language distribution was 50-50 at all grades, so they have overall received less instruction through Spanish.

Academic Achievement in English

The Illinois Goals Assessment Program (IGAP) is administered at every school in Illinois to measure the students' ability to meet state goals for academic achievement. Reading, mathematics, and writing are tested in Grades 3, 6, and 8; science and social sciences are tested in Grades 4 and 7. Limited English proficient students from other countries are not required to take the test until they have received three years of schooling in this country. The 1994-1995 results show that IAMS students are doing far better than their district peers, and in many cases outperforming students in the state as a whole. (See Tables 4.5-4.9.) (Grade level averages include students from both English and Spanish backgrounds, except for newcomers to U.S. schools as mentioned above.)

Table 4.5

Percentage of Students who Meet and Exceed State Goals on the IGAP, Grade 3 (1994-95)

Level	Reading	Math	Writing
IAMS	79	98	96
District	45	64	73
State	74	88	86

Table 4.6

Percentage of Students who Meet and Exceed State Goals on the IGAP, Grade 4 (1994-95)

Level	Social Sciences	Sciences
IAMS	91	87
District	51	68
State	81	89

Table 4.7

Percentage of Students who Meet and Exceed State Goals on the IGAP, Grade 6 (1994-95)

Level	Writing	Math
IAMS	91	82
District	88	64
State	95	85

Table 4.8

Percentage of Students who Meet and Exceed State Goals on the IGAP, Grade 7 (1994-95)

Level	Social Sciences	Sciences
IAMS	84	84
District	73	56
State	88	80

Table 4.9

Percentage of Students who Meet and Exceed State Goals on the IGAP, Grade 8 (1994-95)

Level	Reading	Math	Writing
IAMS	71	78	93
District	49	59	75
State	72	73	88

IAMS students in Grades 4-8 also take the Iowa Test of Basic Skills (ITBS) each year. Students whom individual teachers feel would not be able to perform well on the test due to language limitations are exempt from taking the test for a maximum of three years. The results for the 1995 administration of the ITBS are given in Table 4.10. On the whole, IAMS students were achieving at or just below the national average on all subcomponents at all grade levels.

Table 4.10

1995 Iowa Test of Basic Skills Average Percentiles as Compared to a National Sample

Grade	Reading	Math	Social Studies	Science
4	49	46	45	48
5	46	41	N.A.	N.A.
6	45	47	N.A.	N.A.
7	48	45	N.A	N.A.
8	49	45	50	39

Academic Achievement in Content Studied in Spanish

As indicated in Table 4.11, scores on the 1995 IGAP (given in English) showed that performance in content areas, including those taught in Spanish at IAMS (i.e., math, social studies, science), was generally above average across grade levels, with the exception of the fifth grade's social studies and science scores. (Grade level averages include students from both Spanish and English language backgrounds.)

Table 4.11

IGAP Mathematics, Social Studies, and Science Achievement Scores in Percentiles at each Grade Level (1995)

Grade	Mathematics Achievement in Percentiles	Social Studies Achievement in Percentiles	Science Achievement in Percentiles
3	72.7	N.A.	N.A.
4	72.0	78.1	75.2
5	62.7	32.1	32.1
6	59.9	N.A.	N.A.
7	69.5	N.A.	N.A.
8	60.8	65.2	56.9

Program Impact

IAMS's teachers, program coordinator, and principal were very optimistic about the impact that participation in the program was having and will continue to have on the students. Overall, they believed that the school was accomplishing its goal of developing bilingual students. Despite the shift from a 50-50 model to an 80-20 model, many of those interviewed noted that there was still room for improvement with regard to developing the second language proficiency of native English students. Latecomers to the program (i.e., those who enter the school after first or second grade) also offered a challenge to meeting the school's goals. According to the teachers, strong teacher coordination within an environment that encourages continual examination, adaptation, and improvement helped to meet this challenge and others more effectively, and was a strong factor in the success of this program. The teachers also felt that the program was particularly effective in creating individual and cultural pride, as a result of the school's multicultural emphasis and student-centered curriculum.

All teachers interviewed agreed that IAMS offered a successful two-way bilingual immersion program. Teachers felt these aspects of the program were working particularly well:

- Cooperative learning
- Caring and dedicated teachers
- Small class size
- Respect for all cultures
- Parental involvement
- Student ownership

Teachers felt that some aspects of the program needed work to make the program more effective:

- More Spanish language resource materials
- School-wide coordination (across grades) on instruction (especially in Spanish)
- A reduction in the number of late-entry students, or finding better ways to deal with them
- More exposure to Spanish to improve second language skills of native-English-speaking students

Conclusions

IAMS appeared to be meeting its stated goals of maintaining and developing both the native and second language skills of all of its students. Latecomers notwithstanding, by eighth grade students at IAMS were able to speak, read, and write in Spanish and English. Although the program did not formally assess the oral Spanish abilities of the students, informal assessment was conducted as teacher teams collaborated on a regular basis. This informal assessment has also prompted improvements to the program. For instance, when the school staff determined that the level of student oral Spanish proficiency was not high enough, they altered the program to increase the amount of instructional time in Spanish. This kind of ongoing self-examination, coupled with a willingness to continually revise and refine aspects of the program, was a significant factor in the school's success in meeting its goals.

The fact that IAMS children attend school so regularly was considered to be an indicator of IAMS's success in achieving its goal of creating a caring, cooperative, and accepting school climate, where children from different cultural backgrounds can learn together. The school's 1994 attendance rate was 94.6%, which was higher than the district's and the state's. The intimate involvement of parents in the instructional and administrative components of the school most likely also contribute to creating a safe and comfortable learning environment. This climate is also, no doubt, reinforced by the school atmosphere, which reflects the balance between the English and Spanish languages and diverse cultures, as well a multicultural curriculum that emphasizes studies on the Americas.

On the whole, IAMS students are achieving academically at levels that exceed those of the district and often those of the state, as they are developing bilingual proficiency. A combination of high teacher expectations and active student involvement in the day-to-day issues of their education are likely contributing to the academic success of the IAMS dual language immersion program.

CHAPTER FIVE
Comparisons Across Programs

In this chapter, we will consider all three programs profiled in the preceding chapters, to note their similarities and differences. We will also compare student outcomes, to the extent possible, to determine how the different forms of the model affect language development and academic achievement. The goals of the three programs are similar: to produce students who are bilingual and biliterate, who achieve at or above grade level, and who have positive attitudes toward their peers and other languages (as noted earlier, we have focused on the first two goals in this volume). How the three programs reach these objectives varies to some extent, though they also show remarkable similarities.

Program Background and Population

To begin, it is important to understand the background of the programs and their participants. While two of the programs are now magnet schools and the third has some magnet features, none of them began as a magnet. When they were first implemented, the programs all began as a strand within a school. Each program grew, adding one grade level per year until there was enough demand for the program that it could attract districtwide participation. In two cases, IAMS and River Glen, the programs were incorporated into desegregation plans. None of the programs was begun with Title VII funding, but each school site subsequently received a Title VII grant to further develop its program. The ways in which the programs were initiated differed: Key began as a direct result of the actions of the original principa,; the River Glen principal was approached by the California Department of Education to join a cooperative of schools interested in the model, and IAMS began through the interest of dedicated parents and teachers. In addition, Key was perceived as a foreign language program for gifted students that would also benefit English learners, whereas IAMS and River Glen were developed as bilingual programs that would serve English learners and also benefit native English speakers. As a result, at the district level, the Key program was monitored by the foreign language supervisor, while IAMS and River Glen worked with the bilingual education department.

This range of starting points shows that the program model can be initiated from different perspectives, with or without Title VII funding, and can, but does not have to, serve as a magnet school or as part of a desegregation plan. However, while extra funding is not necessary to begin a program, extra funds are particularly helpful for providing professional development and purchasing instructional materials and library resources in the non-English language. These issues are important for prospective programs to consider in implementing a two-way program.

Table 5.1 presents the populations of the three programs (two whole schools, one program within a school). As Table 5.1 indicates, River Glen and IAMS have high proportions of Hispanic students (68-71%), compared to 48% at Key; Key and River Glen have relatively low percentages of African-American students (2-5%) compared to IAMS (13%). Across all sites, there are few Asian American or Native American students (1%). The percentage of limited English proficient students in the three programs varies, from a low of 35% at IAMS to 40% at Key and 54% at River Glen. However, the meaning of limited English proficient also varied, with Key Spanish speakers beginning the program with higher levels of English proficiency than the River Glen Spanish speakers. Further, the percentage of students eligible for federally funded free and reduced-price lunches ranges from 34% at Key to 47% at River Glen to 60% at IAMS. Finally, some of Key's students, those in the upper grades during our data collection, were screened for entry into this program, which was advertised as a gifted program in its first years of operation. Thus, one might expect higher levels of performance because of the program population. The other two school sites did not conduct any screening. These ethnic, language, and social class variations have important implications for student outcomes as well as for some implementation issues, as will be discussed later.

Two-Way Immersion Education

Table 5.1

Student Population 1994-1995

Program	Key	River Glen	IAMS
Total	318 students	380 students	621 students
Ethnic Breakdown			
Hispanic	48%	68%	71%
European American	46%	29%	15%
African American	5%	2%	13%
Asian/Native American	1%	1%	1%
Free/Reduced-Price Lunch	34%	47%	60%
LEP Population	40%	54%	35%

Across programs, there are slightly different procedures for acceptance of students. None of the programs currently screens students for ability (although Key formerly did), but ethnicity and language background are taken into account to ensure a balanced population. All three programs employ a lottery in some form, because numbers of applicants exceed the number of spaces available. At IAMS, students are selected by a random computer-based lottery at the Pre-K level, taking into account ethnicity (for the desegregation mission) and gender. Prospective River Glen students must register at the district office, select River Glen as their first choice, and be entered into a lottery to obtain a space in the program. At Key, neighborhood students and siblings of students already in the program are automatically enrolled if they apply. Applicants from other areas are placed on a waiting list on a first-come, first-served basis; they are placed into any spaces remaining, using gender and language background balance as selection factors. (In 1993-1994, 10 spaces in the two kindergarten classes were filled from 70 applicants on the waiting list.)

The schools also differ in their acceptance or accommodation of newcomers to the program. At all three schools, English-speaking students are typically allowed to enter the program only at pre-K, K, or first grade (although exceptions do occur). At IAMS, because of the desegregation goals, English-only speakers may be admitted as late as fifth grade, if the percentage of native English-speaking students drops below 15%. However, with a high retention rate, there are few openings at later grades. River Glen Spanish speakers are also rarely admitted into the program at the upper grade levels, as there is usually no space for them. IAMS Spanish-speaking, but not English-speaking, newcomers are incorporated into the two-way program at all grade levels. Key places Spanish-speaking LEP latecomers into another program (High Intensity Language Training, or HILT), but may admit native Spanish speakers with high enough English language skills into the two-way program at any grade level.

Program Design

The three programs differ with respect to their overall design. While River Glen follows a 90-10 model, IAMS adheres to an 80-20 model, and Key to a 50-50 model. Table 5.2 presents the breakdown by grade level of the three programs.

Table 5.2

Program Design by Grade Level and School Site: Percentage of Instruction in Spanish and English

Grade Level	Key	River Glen	IAMS
Kindergarten-First	50-50	90-10	80-20
Second	50-50	85-15	80-20
Third	50-50	80-20	80-20
Fourth-Fifth	50-50	60-40	60-40
Sixth	50-50	50-50	60-40

As Table 5.2 shows, across the three programs, there is variation in the amount of instruction that occurs in each language. In terms of percentages, River Glen and IAMS are more similar, with each providing a greater amount of Spanish instruction in the early grades than Key does. This model resembles the *total immersion* approach from foreign language pedagogy, while the Key School model resembles a *partial immersion* approach. It is important to remember that IAMS began implementing the two-way model with a structure similar to Key's, a 50-50 model, but in 1988 changed to an 80-20 model. Thus, the fifth and sixth graders that we observed began kindergarten (and sixth graders, first grade) in a 50-50 program.

As indicated in Table 5.3, the three programs have different approaches to initial literacy instruction. River Glen teaches both native Spanish and native English speakers to read first in Spanish over the course of Grades K to 2. Then in third grade, all students begin formal reading instruction in English. This contrasts with IAMS, where students learn to read first in their native language (English speakers in English and Spanish speakers in Spanish). Second language reading and writing are introduced in second grade. At Key, all students begin reading in both languages simultaneously, with a focus on their native language.

Table 5.3

Initial Reading Instruction by Grade Level and School Site

Grade Level	Key	River Glen	IAMS
K-First	ALL: English & Spanish	ALL: Spanish	English Proficient: English Spanish Proficient: Spanish
Second			ALL: add L2 (approx.)
Third		ALL: add English	

Contrasting approaches to literacy instruction have implications for student ability to take part in content mastery at their grade level in the language in which they are not reading. For example, at River

Glen, when students are not reading in English during Grades 1 and 2, they cannot be expected to undertake literacy-based activities in English, and thus, their English language arts time is devoted to teacher-directed lessons in literature, drama, storytelling, and music. This contrasts with IAMS, where students read first in their native language. Thus, during Spanish instruction, English speakers would not be expected to participate in literacy-based activities at first, though their literacy skills transfer quickly. Key, on the other hand, has students learn to read in both languages, and literacy activities are part of both English and Spanish instruction for all students. Since many of Key's Spanish speakers enter school with at least moderate proficiency in English, the early introduction of English literacy would not be expected to pose a problem (especially since native language literacy is also developed). At other sites where students begin kindergarten with little or no English proficiency, an immersion into English literacy could be problematic, as noted in the bilingual education literature.

These different approaches to literacy have important implications for student performance and assessment in the two languages. Clearly, students who do not begin reading instruction in English until the later grades will be behind their English-speaking peers who began reading in English in first grade. They will require time to catch up. Similarly, students who begin reading instruction in Spanish will be more likely to maintain grade-level norms in Spanish. How literacy instruction is developed through two languages is critical and must be thought through carefully.

Program Features

Administrative Support and Staffing

All three school sites have demonstrated their success in serving the students in the program; that is why they have long waiting lists and flourish as magnet settings. Although their success and magnet status does not ensure administrative support in the central office, as seen with River Glen, there is clear district support for the Key and IAMS schools, demonstrated by the expansion of the two-way model in each of their districts.

At the school site level, each of the three schools has had strong leadership. The principals have been not only supportive, but they are extremely knowledgeable about the program and its implementation. In addition, each school was fortunate to have a very capable resource teacher or program coordinator. The leadership of the program coordinator was considered vital to the successful implementation and continued development of each program.

Across the three sites, the teachers and staff are very dedicated professionals who constantly strive to provide high quality instruction. Teachers varied, to some extent, across the sites, in their level of bilingual proficiency. At River Glen and IAMS, all teachers have very high levels of Spanish and English proficiency. Key teachers who provided Spanish instruction were fully bilingual, but some teachers who delivered instruction only in English possessed little, if any, proficiency in Spanish. This is a common situation where there are not sufficient teachers with Spanish-speaking proficiency to fully staff the program, and it is an important consideration for implementation. At the early grade levels, students should be able to respond to the teacher in whichever language they can. If Spanish-speaking students do not have the proficiency level to enable them to respond in English to a monolingual English teacher, the program may not adequately support the language needs of all students. An advantage of two-way programs in this regard is the presence of students from both language backgrounds who can help one another and the teacher in such situations. Also, monolingual English teachers may be more easily incorporated in a program where many of the Spanish speakers have some capacity to respond in English when they enter school, which is the case at Key, but this would be inappropriate in a situation like River Glen, where most Spanish speakers enter school with very limited English language ability.

Curriculum

An extremely important feature underlying these and other two-way programs is that the students follow the same curriculum as their peers in English-only classrooms, although they study this curriculum through two languages instead of one. This means that the curriculum

 CARL A. RUDISILL LIBRARY
LENOIR-RHYNE COLLEGE

is never simplified; it is at least as challenging as that in the non-two-way classroom. While all the programs profiled here followed the grade-appropriate curriculum for their state and district, the way in which the curriculum was delivered across languages varied somewhat. (Each program also changed subject/language pairings occasionally from one year to the next, depending on factors like teacher preference, materials availability, and so on.)

As Table 5.4 shows, each program offered language arts in both languages. However, as was stated earlier, there were differences with respect to initial literacy instruction, which influenced what was actually taught during English language arts and Spanish language arts (see previous section). Mathematics instruction was typically given in Spanish in kindergarten through fifth grade at all three schools, although at IAMS, Spanish and English units alternated in Grades 4 through 6. In contrast, the three sites varied according to the language in which science and social studies were taught. In grades K through 5 at Key, English was used to teach social studies (with the exception of first grade during the first year of the study), and science instruction was in Spanish. (In sixth grade, science was taught in English and social studies in Spanish.) The language of instruction for social studies as well as science at River Glen and IAMS varied depending on the grade level, with Spanish used in the earlier grades and both English and Spanish used in the later grades. At River Glen, fourth and fifth grade science was taught in Spanish and social studies was in English, and in sixth grade the subjects and languages were reversed. At IAMS, instruction alternated between the two languages during the year in fourth through sixth grade for both social studies and science.

Thus, the three schools were similar in the early grades (K-3), but varied more in the pairing of language and content in the upper elementary grades. All taught language arts in both languages throughout the grades. All three sites spent considerable time developing an articulated curriculum as well.

Table 5.4[13]

Curriculum Design by Language, Grade Level, and School Site

Grade Level	Science/ Health	Social Studies	Math	Language Arts
K-3	Spanish (I,K, R)	Spanish (I,R) English (K)	Spanish (I,K,R)	Spanish and English (I,K,R)
4-5	Spanish (K,R) Spanish & English (I)	English (K,R) Spanish & English (I)	Spanish (K,R) Spanish & English (I)	Spanish and English (I,K,R)
6	English (K,R) Spanish & English (I)	Spanish (K,R) Spanish & English (I)	Spanish (R) English (K) Spanish & English (I)	Spanish and English (I,K,R)

I=IAMS	K=Key	R=River Glen

The choice of language is, in part, dependent on the materials and curriculum to be taught. However, it is also important to recognize that different subjects may require or provide contexts for the use of different linguistic structures and academic discourse (Lindholm & Cuevas, 1996). The decision to alternate languages for different content areas at IAMS and River Glen was in part to develop the appropriate vocabulary in each language. At Key, much of the instruction was thematic, so that language structures and vocabulary characteristic of various content areas were dealt with in both languages through content integration.

---

[13] Because various teachers may integrate across content areas, the breakdown of language by content is approximate.

Students were engaged in the writing process at all three sites. Thus, teachers were trained in and students were learning the different types of writing and the steps in writing, from pre-writing organizational activities through publishing.

At all three sites, the curriculum and program design were developed to accommodate the needs of the students at that particular site. Each school has been true to the model that they have implemented, regardless of its design or curriculum. However, each has been willing to make changes, as necessary, to further strengthen the program or enhance student outcomes (e.g., IAMS changing from a 50-50 model to an 80-20 model). These changes came about with very careful deliberation about how the changes would affect various components of the model. Thus, the willingness to adapt to student needs must be balanced with a careful understanding of how the changes will affect the new model and student needs. This is an important consideration.

Professional Development

The three school sites are all committed to professional development, and in-service training is an ongoing activity. IAMS stands out for its system of mentoring new teachers and for the autonomy given to teachers in deciding how best to develop themselves professionally. River Glen provides a strong training model that emphasizes understanding the theoretical model, appropriate methodologies for teaching in the two-way model, and articulation across the grade levels. In addition, the principal observes new and experienced teachers and works with them to improve their teaching strategies. All three schools organize teachers into teams for sharing instructional materials and implementing curriculum changes. As exemplified at these sites, professional development should be a priority, particularly for newly implemented two-way programs.

Parent Involvement

All three schools have very supportive parents, as do most two-way programs. Parents volunteer in the classrooms, assist teachers with various tasks, and participate on advisory committees. Furthermore, at times they have had to fight to keep their program in existence. The

IAMS school district operates on the basis of site-based management, so parents there are very active on the Local School Committee, which makes many of the staffing and program decisions at the school. As mentioned earlier, parents were largely responsible for the founding of IAMS as well. Parent involvement has helped these program to grow and flourish. While parent involvement is important in any effective program (Levine & Lezotte, 1995), it is even more essential in two-way programs to assure that they are institutionalized in the district, rather than perceived as a short-term interesting idea. To be most effective, *all* parents must feel that they are welcome in classroom assistance, decision making, and other parent activities.

Learning Environment

Each classroom that was visited displayed a variety of stimulating and colorful materials on bulletin boards and arranged around the classroom. Materials exhibited in the classroom tended to match the language(s) taught in the room. In most classrooms, the teachers had the assistance of classroom aides for at least some portion of the instructional day. Also, each program aimed at balancing the number of English- and Spanish-speaking students in each classroom so that there would be a sufficient number of language models in each language.

At each site, students had access to books and reference and resource materials in English and Spanish in both their classrooms and libraries. All sites had difficulty locating a variety of highly challenging and interesting reading material in Spanish. More advanced multi-chapter books in Spanish that would be interesting to the preteen age group were especially difficult to find. Computers were used at all sites for word processing and other educational applications in the two languages.

Instructional Practices

Separation of Languages

While all three sites believed in separating the languages for instruction, there was a difference in how stringently the policy of not mixing languages was adhered to. At River Glen and Key, teachers strictly followed the policy of no language mixing in the classroom, and language mixing was never observed in the classroom. In the early grades, students were allowed to respond in their native language, but were encouraged to use the instructional language in their responses. Teachers, however, did not vary the language of instruction. By the upper grades, students were expected to do all of their individual, group, and whole-class discussions and work in the language of the content instruction. As noted in the site descriptions, however, many of the older students (Grades 4-6) displayed a strong preference for English, particularly in peer interactions. Supportive instructional materials and textbooks were always selected to be consistent with the language of instruction.

IAMS was somewhat less strict about language separation, with allowance of occasional translations to assist students in the classroom. Like River Glen and Key, IAMS allowed students in the primary grades to express themselves in whatever language they could and increasingly expected them to respond in the language of instruction in the upper grade levels. At Key and IAMS, a lack of content texts in Spanish occasionally led to English-medium textbooks being used for content lessons in Spanish.

In general, there was considerable separation of languages for content instruction. Most teachers worked hard to assure that students developed the content in the appropriate language. This focus on language separation is important. In some school sites, when a student does not understand the content or instructions, the teacher or instructional assistants translate from the instructional language to the student's primary language in an effort to help them. In these situations, students learn that they do not need to learn the second language, because if they act lost enough, the teacher or instructional assistant will translate for them. Thus, for the most part, the teachers at these sites felt that the best strategy was to keep the languages as separate as possible. If translation were needed, a student peer could do the translation, but that was usually a last resort. (More will be said about this in the next section.)

Making Content Comprehensible

At all three sites, there were times at all grade levels when at least one or two students did not understand the content. As in any classroom where students do not understand the content (even in their native language), the teachers used a variety of measures to assure that the language and content were comprehensible to the students. To assist in this effort, various resources were employed, including overhead projectors and computers, Venn diagrams, brainstorming, drama and acting, and concrete contextual references (visuals, realia).

Teachers also used a number of instructional strategies to make language comprehensible. These encompassed sheltering, student-teacher modeling, realia, TPR, illustrations, and rephrasing to improve comprehension and develop vocabulary. Teachers also monitored student comprehension through interactive means such as comprehension checks, clarification requests, a variety of questioning types, paraphrasing, providing definitions, expansion, scaffolding, and modeling.

Sometimes, even after using these various strategies, a student would not understand the content or instructions under discussion. During these interactions where it was clear that a student was not comprehending the teacher, often other students would spontaneously translate for the student or say it in another way that would assist the student. As a last resort, teachers would have a student translate for another student. However, to assure that some students did not become dependent on translation, teachers tried to use other strategies listed above to help the students figure out the concept in the language of instruction before resorting to translation.

Language Development Strategies

As is typical of immersion teachers, most teachers at the three sites were likely to either let linguistic errors pass if the utterance was intelligible or model the appropriate utterance back to the student. When students did make an error, the teachers typically focused on the content as opposed to the structure of the student's response. Teachers rarely overtly corrected or had the students correct their language-based errors. Two of the sites expressed concern about persistent non-native usage in Spanish and are exploring means of increasing the focus on language form in meaningful contexts to address this concern. Key was the only program that had started overt teaching of grammar during language arts. River Glen is beginning to phase in grammar instruction as an integral part of their program.

Across the sites, the writing process was used to develop students' ability to write in the two languages. Thus, there were contexts in which students did not have their written work corrected, but in other contexts, they went through the process of editing and publishing their work. Throughout this process, they were able to focus on the grammatical and spelling errors in their written work.

Finally, teachers also tried to use as much challenging material as possible to increase the language skills of the students. Two common strategies were to build vocabulary skills through a variety of activities and discussions and to model sophisticated language. Many teachers reported that they would reword or rephrase students' utterances if they grasped the concept but were having difficulty in expressing it verbally.

Student Grouping

At the three schools, students participated in heterogeneous groups for cooperative interactive learning activities. Each school felt that the heterogeneous nature of the grouping was essential for the success of the two-way model; that is, students must have the opportunity to work collaboratively and use language with each other in order to promote higher levels of second language proficiency as well as positive cross-cultural attitudes.

Student Language Development and Academic Outcomes

A Comment on Measures

In the course of collecting the descriptive information about the school sites, we attempted to be as unobtrusive and undemanding as possible. In some cases, we requested particular measures, or types of measures, to assess outcomes (especially language-related), but for achievement and other student and program data, we relied on what could be made available from the site (described in the preceding chapters). As a result, we do not have identical assessments at identical grade levels to allow for direct comparison of student outcomes across all three sites. In the following sections, the available data will be discussed and compared when possible.

Separation of Languages

At the different school sites, across different classroom situations, the use of English among students during Spanish time was usually tolerated. Students were encouraged and expected to speak Spanish during Spanish time and were usually reminded to use Spanish if they were using English. At the upper grade levels, however, when they had the opportunity to choose a language, students often spoke in English. Despite this preference for English, students showed high levels of comprehension skills during classroom lecture, discussion, and work in both Spanish and English. During English instruction, there was seldom any use of Spanish by students.

Oral Language Development

Data on language proficiency were limited across the sites. None of the sites had measures that assess first language *development* (e.g., *Woodcock Johnson Language Proficiency Battery*). No oral language proficiency data were available for IAMS. Common assessment tools were used at Key and River Glen to examine second language development. The *Student Oral Language Observation Matrix* (SOLOM), upon which the *Student Oral Proficiency Rating* (SOPR) was based, and the *Language Assessment Scales* (LAS) were used at both sites.

Table 5.5 presents the average SOLOM/SOPR ratings given by teachers to the students in Spanish. A review of Table 5.5 shows the Spanish scores were very high, with average scores of 14.0 to 24.7 (out of a possible 25). The percentage of students who obtained a score of 19 or better, the rating considered to indicate fluency, is also shown.

While the SOLOM and SOPR are very similar measures, they both are teacher rating instruments. Even when teachers are carefully trained to use the SOLOM/SOPR, ratings can fluctuate to some extent across teachers, which can affect the reliability. Ratings may also be influenced by social expectations. Because the United States is an English-speaking country, it is expected that students will speak English. Thus, teachers may rate English and Spanish speakers appropriately in English—with higher standards and comparisons to English monolinguals, as dictated by the instrument. Furthermore, because Spanish speakers have Spanish as their dominant language, many teachers have high expectations for their Spanish proficiency, even to the extent of giving them low rating as kindergartners and first graders if they lack some grammatical structures or vocabulary. In contrast, some teachers tend to overrate English speakers' Spanish proficiency, because they are so impressed that the English speakers can speak Spanish. The category definitions on these instruments allow for variable interpretation, as well, leading some teachers to give students a higher score (5, native speaker level) than they may deserve. These are important factors to consider in reviewing the ratings shown in Table 5.5

Table 5.6 provides *Language Assessment Scales* information about English oral proficiency for Spanish speakers at Key and River Glen. As Table 5.6 indicates, the percentage of students designated as fluent at River Glen (according to grade-sensitive levels provided in the scoring instructions for the LAS) was 50% in Grade 1, 74% in Grade 2, 95% in Grade 3, and 100% in Grades 4 through 6. At Key, LAS scores were available only for third graders, where 100% of Spanish speakers were designated as fluent in English. According to the LAS, then, the River Glen 90-10 and Key 50-50 programs produced fairly similar mean scores at third grade (M =79 at River Glen, 88 at Key), and almost all students scored as fluent in English (95% at River Glen, 100% at Key).

Table 5.5

Average SOLOM/SOPR Scores in Spanish by School Site and Grade Level, 1995

Grade Level and Language Background	Percent Fluent		Average Score	
	River Glen	Key	River Glen	Key
First Grade:				
Spanish Speakers	100%	88%	24.7	23.0
English Speakers	60%	21%	21.6	14.0
Second Grade:				
Spanish Speakers	100%	100%	24.7	23.4
English Speakers	47%	21%	18.4	16.4
Third Grade:				
Spanish Speakers	100%	N/A	24.4	N/A
English Speakers	77%		19.5	
Fourth Grade:				
Spanish Speakers	100%	100%	23.8	24.5
English Speakers	95%	65%	22.2	19.8
Fifth Grade:				
Spanish Speakers	100%	100%	24.2	24.0
English Speakers	100%	43%	23.7	19.7

Table 5.6

English LAS Results for Spanish Speakers

Grade Level	Percent Fluent		Average Score	
	River Glen (1995)	Key (1994)	River Glen (1995)	Key (1994)
First Grade	50%	N/A	62	N/A
Second Grade	74%	N/A	73	N/A
Third Grade	95%	100%	79	88
Fourth Grade	100%	N/A	80	N/A
Fifth Grade	100%	N/A	91	N/A
Sixth Grade	100%	N/A	87	N/A

The results from the LAS and the SOLOM/SOPR are interesting to compare across the Key and River Glen sites as these are the two that differ most in their model, with River Glen's 90-10 model and Key's 50-50 model. From this cross-sectional perspective, the English-speaking students across grade levels show progress in Spanish oral language skills along with maintenance of high oral language proficiency in English. Spanish-speakers across grade levels show development in Spanish along with impressive gains in oral English language proficiency. By third grade, the majority of Spanish-speaking students in both programs scored as fluent in English on the LAS. At River Glen, a majority of the English-speaking students scored as fluent in Spanish (on the SOLOM) by third grade as well, while at Key, the level of Spanish proficiency (rated on the SOPR) was slightly lower.

Looking at the average scores, these data would suggest that English speakers do not become quite as proficient in Spanish in a 50-50 program as in a 90-10 program, but they do show high levels of second language development. The lack of data in Spanish other than the SOLOM/SOPR does not allow us to compare the Spanish proficiency of the students fully (given the limitations of a single teacher rating). However, the results point to strong progress in second language learning among all students in both programs.

Academic Achievement

Reading and Writing Achievement in Spanish. Table 5.7 shows the students' average percentiles from the *La Prueba* reading and writing achievement subtests for third through sixth graders at River Glen and IAMS. (Key has no standardized achievement testing in Spanish.) These two sites have similar models (River Glen 90-10; IAMS 80-20). As Table 5.7 indicates, performance was comparable across the sites, with percentiles at or above average (average defined as performance at the 50th percentile) in reading and writing achievement.

Table 5.7

Spanish Reading and Writing Achievement Scores, 1995

Grade Level	Reading Achievement in Percentiles		Writing Achievement in Percentiles	
	River Glen (90-10)	IAMS (80-20)	River Glen (90-10)	IAMS (80-20)
Third Grade	54	69	69	67
Fourth Grade	60	65	68	70
Fifth Grade	50	61	69	62
Sixth Grade	57	61	60	53

Mathematics, Social Studies, and Science Achievement in Spanish. Table 5.8 presents the percentiles from the *La Prueba* achievement test in Spanish in the areas of mathematics, social studies, and science for River Glen and IAMS third through sixth graders. Table 5.8 shows that mathematics, social studies, and science performance was average to high for all grades (with the exception of IAMS fifth graders in social studies and science). Again, the results across the two schools with similar models were remarkably parallel (except for the IAMS fifth graders).

Table 5.8

Spanish Mathematics, Social Studies, and Science Achievement Scores, 1995

Grade Level	Math Achievement in Percentiles		Social Studies Achievement in Percentiles		Science Achievement in Percentiles	
	River Glen (90-10)	IAMS (80-20)	River Glen (90-10)	IAMS (80-20)	River Glen (90-10)	IAMS (80-20)
Third Grade	68	73	69	--	68	--
Fourth Grade	72	72	67	78	69	75
Fifth Grade	59	63	76	32	58	32
Sixth Grade	61	60	54	--	64	--

Reading, Language, and Mathematics Achievement in English. Table 5.9 displays the students' average percentiles from the ITBS (Key, IAMS) and CTBS (River Glen) reading, language, and mathematics achievement subtests for fourth graders. (It is important to remember that no students began reading instruction in English at River Glen until third grade, and Spanish speakers at IAMS did not read in English until second grade.) As Table 5.9 illustrates, the River Glen and IAMS students scored in the average range while Key students scored in the high range.

Table 5.9

English Reading, Language and Mathematics Achievement Scores in Percentiles for the Fourth Grade, 1995

School	Reading Achievement in Percentiles	Language Achievement in Percentiles	Math Achievement in Percentiles
River Glen (90-10)	44	52	54
IAMS (80-20)	49	N/A	46
Key (50-50)	89	79	93

Conclusions

In this chapter, we have attempted to compare the characteristics and outcomes of the three two-way programs described earlier. It is clear that there are a number of similarities across the three sites. First, all programs conscientiously adhered to their model, worked to implement it correctly, and carefully articulated it across the grade levels. Second, each program had administrative staff (including a program coordinator) who were knowledgeable about the two-way model and who supported or guided the program toward its success as an education program within the school and district. Third, there were highly proficient and very capable teachers at each site who have received considerable professional development so that they understood important components of the model, including second language development and good instructional strategies (though many of the River Glen teachers were new to the program model and new to teaching in the period under observation). Fourth, in observing the classrooms, it appeared that teachers were using similar instructional strategies for making language and content comprehensible to the students and for developing language skills. Fifth, the learning environments surrounding the students shared many features and heterogeneous grouping of students in the classroom was common in all sites. Thus, there was considerable similarity in many of the major features of the three programs.

The predominant variations across the sites related to the ratio of Spanish to English and the language of initial literacy. Key and IAMS began their implementation with a 50-50 program model, but IAMS changed to an 80-20 model after deciding that the Spanish proficiency of the students was not high enough. Thus, their model currently resembles more closely the River Glen 90-10 model. There did not appear to be major differences in long-term student outcomes related to variations on language distribution or literacy instruction, according to the data we were able to collect.

These variations in program models reflect both differences in community needs as well as the populations served by the schools. At Key, the model originated as an enrichment program for gifted students, and some students were screened out who did not meet certain levels of language and conceptual development. Also, because of the sociolinguistic context, many of the Spanish speakers in Key's program arrive at school with some proficiency in English. As a result, their approach to literacy instruction in both languages is very appropriate. Also, their high levels of achievement in English attest to a strong English-language base and perhaps a more select student population. In contrast, at IAMS, there is a much larger population of free and reduced-price lunch students (60%) from various ethnic groups (including a larger percentage of English-speaking minority students). Their strategy for beginning literacy instruction in the primary language appears to fit this context. River Glen students are a combination of largely middle-class, English-speaking, European-American and Latino students and Spanish speakers, most of whom are free or reduced-price lunch participants and began the program with few, if any, skills in English. Thus, this context may be quite appropriate for developing initial literacy instruction in Spanish. Understanding the population to be served is certainly an important prerequisite in determining which model may be most effective at a particular school site.

Finally, it is important to recognize the limitations in comparing outcomes across the three school sites. First, there were not identical sources of data across all three sites. Second, when there were comparable outcomes, they were usually based on slightly different measures (SOPR at Key vs. SOLOM at River Glen; ITBS at Key vs. CTBS at River Glen). Further, because Key had achievement data only for fourth grade, appropriate comparisons could not be made at the sixth grade level, when scores may have been higher for the 90-10 and 80-20 model because of increased English instruction. At the fourth grade level, Spanish speakers at both sites, as well as English speakers at River Glen, had been reading in English for only two years. Thus, these scores may make the 50-50 model appear more successful than the 90-10 or 80-20 model. Other evaluation data have pointed to substantial increases in English achievement test scores in 90-10 programs by sixth or seventh grade (Lindholm, 1996). More unfortunate is the lack of any comparative achievement data for the 50-50 versus 90-10 and 80-20 models. Key did not do any standardized student testing in Spanish. Fortunately, IAMS and River Glen used the same instrument for assessing Spanish achievement. Their scores were remarkably similar, with students scoring average to high in reading, writing, mathematics, social studies, and science.

Even when the measures were exactly the same (*La Prueba* at River Glen and IAMS), the student populations varied across the sites. These student variations are very critical to understand and deserve closer examination. It is not clear to what extent home environment (including parent level of education; educational books at home; parental assistance with homework; access to technology and other educational experiences), language resources (such as whether the child began as non-English or limited English proficient and the level of English proficiency of the parents), and student characteristics (including giftedness) varied across the three sites. Considerable research has documented the effects of these variables on student achievement (Darling-Hammond, 1995; Knapp & Woolverton, 1995; Olneck, 1995). Research clearly shows that whether a model works at a particular school site depends, among other things, on the student population and on community needs and characteristics (Levine & Lezotte, 1995).

In conclusion, the results from all three sites are positive and demonstrate that two-way immersion programs present a promising and exciting model for promoting bilingualism, biliteracy, and acquisition of average to high levels of content area knowledge for both English and Spanish speakers. While there are some variations across the three sites, each works well with its population in promoting bilingualism, biliteracy, and academic achievement. Two-way immersion programs, then, offer our society the opportunity to profit from the growing diversity in our schools and help all our students achieve the high standards we have set for them. Learning to work, play, and speak with people from diverse linguistic and cultural backgrounds will make it possible for our children to participate more fully and confidently in an increasingly shrinking world.

References

Arlington Public Schools. (1992). *Curriculum guide/units of study, two-way partial immersion program, F.S. Key Elementary School*. Arlington, VA: Author.

Barfield, S. (1995). *Review of the ninth year of the partial immersion program at Key Elementary School, Arlington, VA, 1994-95*. Washington, DC: Center for Applied Linguistics.

Barfield, S., & Rhodes, N. (1994). *Review of the eighth year of the partial immersion program at Key Elementary School, Arlington, VA, 1993-94*. Washington, DC: Center for Applied Linguistics.

Brinton, D., Snow, M., & Wesche, M. (1989). *Content-based second language instruction*. New York: Newbury House.

Chamot, A., & O'Malley, M. (1994). *The CALLA handbook: Implementing the cognitive academic language learning approach*. Reading, MA: Addison-Wesley.

Christian, D. 1996. Two-way immersion education: Students learning through two languages. *The Modern Language Journal, 80*(1), 66-76.

Christian, D., & Whitcher, A. (1995). *Directory of two-way bilingual programs in the U.S.* (rev. ed.). Santa Cruz, CA and Washington, DC: National Center for Research on Cultural Diversity and Second Language Learning.

Collier, V. (1992). A synthesis of studies examining long-term language-minority student data on academic achievement. *Bilingual Research Journal, 16*(1, 2), 187-212.

Craig, B. (1995). *Two-way foreign language programs: A handbook for parents and teachers*. Arlington, VA: Author. (ERIC Document Reproduction Service No. ED 384 239)

Crandall, J. (Ed.). (1995). *ESL through content area instruction.* McHenry, IL and Washington, DC: Delta Systems and Center for Applied Linguistics.

Cummins, J. (1984). Linguistic interdependence among Japanese and Vietnamese immigrant children. In C. Rivera (Ed.), *Communicative competence approaches to language proficiency assessment: Research applications.* Avon, England: Multilingual Matters.

Darling-Hammond, L. (1995). Inequality and access to knowledge. In J.A. Banks & C.A. McGee Banks (Eds.), *Handbook of research on multicultural education* (pp. 465-483). New York: MacMillan.

Day, E.M., & Shapson, S.M. (1996). *Studies in immersion education.* Clevedon, England: Multilingual Matters.

Genesee, F. (1987). *Learning through two languages: Studies of immersion and bilingual education.* Cambridge, MA: Newbury House.

Genesee, F. (1992). Second/foreign language immersion and at-risk English-speaking children. *Foreign Language Annals, 25*(3), 199-213.

Hakuta, K. (1987). Degree of bilingualism and cognitive ability in mainland Puerto Rican children. *Child Development, 58,* 1372-1388.

Hakuta, K. (1990). *Bilingualism and bilingual education: A research perspective.* (Focus: Occasional Papers in Bilingual Education, Spring 1990). Washington, DC: National Clearinghouse for Bilingual Education.

Hakuta, K., & Gould, L. (1987). Synthesis of research on bilingual education. *Educational Leadership, 44*(6), 38-45.

Harley, B. (1993). Instructional strategies and SLA in early French immersion. *Studies in Second Language Acquisition, 15,* 245-259.

Harley, B., Allen, P., Cummins, J., & Swain, M. (1990). *The development of second language proficiency.* Cambridge: Cambridge University Press.

Knapp, M.S., & Woolverton, S. (1995). Social class and schooling. In J.A. Banks & C.A. McGee Banks (Eds.), *Handbook of research on multicultural education* (pp. 548-569). New York: MacMillan.

Krashen, S. (1991). *Bilingual education: A focus on current research*. (Focus: Occasional Papers in Bilingual Education, Spring 1991). Washington, DC: National Clearinghouse for Bilingual Education.

Lambert, W., & Cazabon, M. (1994). *Students' views of the AMIGOS program* (Research Rep. No. 11). Santa Cruz, CA and Washington, DC: National Center for Research on Cultural Diversity and Second Language Learning. (ERIC Document Reproduction Service No. ED 390 248)

Lambert, W., & Tucker, G.R. (1972). *Bilingual education of children: The St. Lambert experiment*. Rowley, MA: Newbury House.

Levine, D.U., & Lezotte, L.W. (1995). Effective schools research. In J.A. Banks & C.A. McGee Banks (Eds.), *Handbook of research on multicultural education* (pp. 525-547). New York: MacMillan.

Lindholm, K. (1987). *Directory of bilingual immersion programs: Two-way bilingual education for language minority and majority students*. Los Angeles: University of California at Los Angeles, Center for Language Education and Research.

Lindholm, K. (1994). Promoting positive cross-cultural attitudes and perceived competence in culturally and linguistically diverse classrooms. In R.A. DeVillar, C.J. Faltis, & J.P. Cummins, (Eds.), *Cultural diversity in schools: From rhetoric to practice*. Albany: State University of New York Press.

Lindholm, K. (1996, April). *Evaluation of academic achievement in two-way bilingual immersion programs*. Paper presented at the annual meeting of the American Educational Research Association, New York.

Lindholm, K., & Cuevas, J. (1996). *Teacher talk and student responses in two-way bilingual immersion classrooms*. Unpublished manuscript, San José State University.

Met, M. (1991). Learning language through content; learning content through language. *Foreign Language Annals, 24*(4), 281-295.

Mohan, B. (1986). *Language and content*. Reading, MA: Addison-Wesley.

Olneck, M.R. (1995). Immigrants and education. In J.A. Banks & C.A. McGee Banks (Eds.), *Handbook of research on multicultural education* (pp. 310-327). New York: MacMillan.

Olsen, R.E.W.-B., & Leone, B. (1994). Sociocultural processes in academic, cognitive, and language development. *TESOL Matters, 4*(3), 1-18.

Snow, C. (1987). Beyond conversation: Second language learners' acquisition of description and explanation. In J. Lantolf & A. Labarca (Eds.), *Research in second language learning: Focus on the classroom* (pp. 3-16). Norwood, NJ: Ablex.

Snow, C. (1994, March 6). *Learning to read a second time: Influence of L1 and L2 oral proficiency.* Paper presented at the annual meeting of the American Association for Applied Linguistics, Baltimore, MD.

Snow, M., Met, M., & Genesee, F. (1989). A conceptual framework for the integration of language and content in second/foreign language instruction. *TESOL Quarterly, 23*, 201-217.

Spanos, G. (1990). On the integration of language and content instruction. *Annual Review of Applied Linguistics, 10*, 227-240.

Swain, M., & Lapkin, S. (1985). *Evaluating bilingual education: A Canadian case study.* Clevedon, England: Multilingual Matters.

Tucker, G.R. (1990). Cognitive and social correlates of additive bilinguality. In J.E. Alatis (Ed.), *Georgetown University Round Table on Languages and Linguistics.* Washington, DC: Georgetown University Press.

Recommended Reading

Cazabon, M., Lambert, W.E., & Hall, G. (1993). *Two-way bilingual education: A progress report on the Amigos program* (Research Rep. No. 7). Santa Cruz, CA and Washington, DC: National Center for Research on Cultural Diversity and Second Language Learning.

Christian, D. (1996). Two-way immersion education: Students learning through two languages. *The Modern Language Journal, 80*(1), 66-76.

Collier, V. (1995). Acquiring a second language for school. *Directions in Language and Education, 1*(4). Washington, DC: National Clearinghouse for Bilingual Education. (ERIC Document Reproduction Service No. ED 394 301)

Genesee, F. (1987). *Learning through two languages: Studies of immersion and bilingual education.* Cambridge, MA: Newbury House.

Lambert, W., & Cazabon, M. (1994). *Students' view of the Amigos program* (Research Rep. No. 11). Santa Cruz, CA and Washington, DC: National Center for Research on Cultural Diversity and Second Language Learning.

Lindholm, K. (1990). Bilingual immersion education: Criteria for program development. In A. Padilla, H. Fairchild, & C. Valadez (Eds.), *Bilingual education: Issues and strategies.* Newbury Park, CA: Sage.

Lindholm, K. (1992). Two-way bilingual/immersion education: Theory, conceptual issues, and pedagogical implications. In R. Padilla & A. Benavides (Eds.), *Critical perspectives on bilingual education research.* Tucson, AZ: Bilingual Review/Press.

Lindholm, K. (1993). Un modelo educacional de éxito para estudiantes inmigrantes de origen latino [A successful educational model for Latino immigrant students]. *Revista de psicología social y personalidad [Journal of Social Psychology and Personality]*, *9*, 85-94.

Lindholm, K. (1994). Promoting positive cross-cultural attitudes and perceived competence in culturally and linguistically diverse classrooms. In R.A. DeVillar, C.J. Faltis, & J.P. Cummins (Eds.), *Cultural diversity in schools: From rhetoric to practice* (pp. 189-206). Albany, NY: State University of New York Press.

Lindholm, K., & Aclan, Z. (1991). Bilingual proficiency as a bridge to academic achievement: Results from bilingual/immersion programs. *Journal of Education, 173(2)*, 99-113.

National Center for Research on Cultural Diversity and Second Language Learning. (1994). *Two-way bilingual education programs in practice: A national and local perspective. ERIC Digest.* Washington, DC: ERIC Clearinghouse on Languages and Linguistics. (ERIC Document Reproduction Service No. ED 379 915)

Tucker, G.R. (1990). Cognitive and social correlates of additive bilinguality. In J.E. Alatis (Ed.), *Georgetown University Round Table on Languages and Linguistics.* Washington, DC: Georgetown University Press.

SOLOM Teacher Observation
Student Oral Language Observation Matrix

Student's Name _____ Grade _____ Signature _____

Language observed _____ Date _____

		1	2	3	4	5
A.	Comprehension	Cannot be said to understand even simple conversation.	Has great difficulty following what is said. Can comprehend only "social conversation" spoken slowly and with frequent repetitions.	Understands most of what is said at slower-than-normal speed with repetitions.	Understands nearly everything at normal speed, although occasional repetition may be necessary.	Understands everyday conversation and normal classroom discussions without difficulty.
B.	Fluency	Speech is so halting and fragmentary as to make conversation virtually impossible.	Usually hesitant; often forced into silence by language limitations.	Speech in everyday conversation and classroom discussion frequently disrupted by the student's search for the correct manner of expression.	Speech in everyday conversation and classroom discussions generally fluent, with occasional lapses while the student searches for the correct manner of expression.	Speech in everyday conversation and classroom discussions fluent and effortless, approximating that of a native speaker.
C.	Vocabulary	Vocabulary limitations so extreme as to make conversation virtually impossible.	Misuse of words and very limited vocabulary; comprehension quite difficult.	Student frequently uses the wrong words; conversation somewhat limited because of inadequate vocabulary.	Student occasionally uses inappropriate terms and/or must rephrase ideas because of lexical inadequacies.	Use of vocabulary and idioms approximate that of a native speaker.
D.	Pronunciation	Pronunciation problems so severe as to make speech virtually unintelligible.	Very hard to understand because of pronunciation problems. Must frequently repeat in order to make himself or herself understood.	Pronunciation problems necessitate concentration on the part of the listener and occasionally lead to misunderstanding.	Always intelligible, though one is conscious of a definite accent and occasional inappropriate intonation patterns.	Pronunciation and intonation approximate that of a native speaker.
E.	Grammar	Errors in grammar and word order so severe as to make speech virtually unintelligible.	Grammar and word-order errors make comprehension difficult. Must often rephrase and/or restrict himself or herself to basic patterns.	Makes frequent errors of grammar and word-order which occasionally obscure meaning.	Occasionally makes grammatical and/or word-order errors which do not obscure meaning.	Grammatical usage and word order approximate that of a native speaker.

Based on your observation of the student, indicate with an "X" across the square in each category which best describes the student's abilities.

adix   125

Student Oral Proficiency Rating*

Score _____

Student's Name _____ Grade _____ Language Observed _____

School _____ City _____ State _____

Rated by _____ Date _____

DIRECTIONS: For each of the 5 categories below at the left, mark an "X" across the box that best describes the student's abilities.

	LEVEL 1	LEVEL 2	LEVEL 3	LEVEL 4	LEVEL 5
A. Comprehension	Cannot understand even simple conversation.	Has great difficulty following what is said. Can comprehend only "social conversation" spoken slowly and with frequent repetitions.	Understands most of what is said at slower-than-normal speed with repetitions.	Understands nearly everything at normal speed, although occasional repetition may be necessary.	Understands everyday conversation and normal classroom discussions without difficulty.
B. Fluency	Speech is so halting and fragmentary as to make conversation virtually impossible.	Usually hesitant; often forced into silence by language limitations.	Speech in everyday communication and classroom discussion is frequently disrupted by the student's search for the correct manner of expression.	Speech in everyday communication and classroom discussion is generally fluent, with occasional lapses while the student searches for the correct manner of expression.	Speech in everyday conversation and in classroom discussion is fluent and effortless, approximating that of a native speaker.
C. Vocabulary	Vocabulary limitations are so extreme as to make conversation virtually impossible.	Misuse of words and very limited vocabulary make comprehension quite difficult.	Frequently uses the wrong words; conversation somewhat limited because of inadequate vocabulary.	Occasionally uses inappropriate terms or must rephrase ideas because of inadequate vocabulary.	Use of vocabulary and idioms approximates that of a native speaker.
D. Pronunciation	Pronunciation problems so severe as to make speech virtually unintelligible.	Very hard to understand because of pronunciation problems. Must frequently repeat in order to be understood.	Pronunciation problems necessitate concentration on the part of the listener and occasionally lead to misunderstanding.	Always intelligible, though one is conscious of a definite accent and occasional inappropriate intonation patterns.	Pronunciation and intonation approximate a native speaker's.
E. Grammar	Errors in grammar and word order so severe as to make speech virtually unintelligible.	Grammar and word order errors make comprehension difficult. Must often rephrase or restrict what is said to basic patterns.	Makes frequent errors of grammar and word order which occasionally obscure meaning.	Occasionally makes grammatical or word order errors which do not obscure meaning.	Grammatical usage and word order approximate a native speaker's.

*This form is an adaptation of the Student Oral Language Observation Matrix (SOLOM) developed by the San Jose (California) Unified School District

About the Authors

Donna Christian is President of the Center for Applied Linguistics (CAL) in Washington, DC. She has worked with CAL since 1974, focusing on the role of language in education, including issues of second language education and dialect diversity. She is active in research, program evaluation, and teacher development and currently directs a program of research on two-way bilingual immersion. She has published numerous books and articles on language diversity, language education, and the education of minority students in the United States. Dr. Christian received a Ph.D. in sociolinguistics from Georgetown University.

Christopher L. Montone is a Research Assistant at the Center for Applied Linguistics. He holds a Master of Arts degree in teaching English as a second language/bilingual education from Georgetown University and an M.A. in Latin American Studies from Tulane University. Mr. Montone's research, publications, and conference presentations have focused on two-way immersion programs and the integration of language and content for instruction. He is currently investigating two-way immersion program articulation issues and newcomer programs in secondary schools.

Kathryn J. Lindholm is Professor of Child Development at San Jose State University. She received her Ph.D. in developmental psychology from the University of California, Los Angeles. Dr. Lindholm's research interests are focused on assessing the effectiveness of two-way bilingual education program models. She serves as a consultant to many school districts, the California State Department of Education, and the Center for Applied Linguistics. She has authored or co-authored numerous journal articles and chapters on child bilingualism, two-way bilingual education, and multicultural themes in child development.

Isolda Carranza is Associate Professor at the National University of Córdoba (Argentina). Her main area of specialization is oral discourse in face-to-face interaction. She has studied conversational discourse markers in Spanish and wrote her doctoral dissertation on argumentation and ideological outlook in storytelling. She obtained fellowships from the American Association of University Women and Georgetown University to pursue her Ph.D. in linguistics. Prior to accepting her current post in Argentina, Dr. Carranza worked at the Center for Applied Linguistics in Washington, DC, where her research focused on classroom and school ethnography.

Language in Education: Theory and Practice

The Educational Resources Information Center (ERIC), which is supported by the Office of Educational Research and Improvement of the U.S. Department of Education, is a nationwide system of information centers, each responsible for a given educational level or field of study. ERIC's basic objective is to make developments in educational research, instruction, and teacher training readily accessible to educators and members of related professions.

The ERIC Clearinghouse on Languages and Linguistics (ERIC/CLL), one of the specialized information centers in the ERIC system, is operated by the Center for Applied Linguistics (CAL) and is specifically responsible for the collection and dissemination of information on research in languages and linguistics and on the application of research to language teaching and learning.

In 1989, CAL was awarded a contract to expand the activities of ERIC/CLL through the establishment of an adjunct ERIC clearinghouse, the National Clearinghouse for ESL Literacy Education (NCLE). NCLE's specific focus is literacy education for language minority adults and out-of-school youth.

ERIC/CLL and NCLE commission recognized authorities in languages, linguistics, adult literacy education, and English as a second language (ESL) to write about current issues in these fields. Monographs, intended for educators, researchers, and others interested in language education, are published under the series title, *Language in Education: Theory and Practice* (LIE). The *LIE* series includes practical guides for teachers, state-of-the-art papers, research reviews, and collected reports.

For further information on the ERIC system, ERIC/CLL, or NCLE, contact either clearinghouse at the Center for Applied Linguistics, 4646 40th Street, NW, Washington, DC 20016-1859.

271 B1 FM 43
06/16/00 39255 SELB